AKRON-CANTON BASEBALL HERITAGE

Kent State University, located 15 miles northeast of Akron, has produced numerous professional baseball players. Seen here (left to right) are stars Thurman Munson and Rich Rollins honoring their former Kent State teammate Gene Michael before a 1970 ball game. (Courtesy of the Cleveland Press Collection, Cleveland State University Special Collections.)

On the font cover: Akron native Thurman Munson is seen during his playing days at Kent State University. (Courtesy of Kent State University Archives.)

On the back cover: Akron Aeros are in action at their home stadium, Canal Park. (Courtesy of the Holbert collection.)

Cover background: The inaugural game of the Goodyear Industrial team was at Seiberling Field on July 14, 1929. (Courtesy of the University of Akron Archives.)

AKRON-CANTON BASEBALL HERITAGE

Thomas Maroon, Margaret Maroon, and Craig Holbert

ARCADIA PUBLISHING

ISBN 978-0-7385-5113-5

Published by Arcadia Publishing
Charleston, South Carolina

Printed in the United States of America

Library of Congress Catalog Card Number: 2007920803

For all general information contact Arcadia Publishing at:
Telephone 843-853-2070
Fax 843-853-0044
E-mail sales@arcadiapublishing.com
For customer service and orders:
Toll-Free 1-888-313-2665

Visit us on the Internet at www.arcadiapublishing.com

To our families, for all of their love and support throughout the years.

CONTENTS

ACKNOWLEDGMENTS

There are many groups and individuals whose contributions made this book possible. Specifically, the authors would first like to thank the following for providing vintage photographs of baseball in the Akron-Canton area: William Barrow and Lynn M. Duchez Bycko at Cleveland State University Special Collections; Gary Harwood, chief photographer of Kent State University; Stephen Paschen at the Kent State University Archives; and John Miller and Oliver Corrigan at the University of Akron Archives. The authors would also like to thank Ted Hardy and the Greater Akron Baseball Hall of Fame for supplying both photographs as well as information on local players.

Finally, the authors would like to thank Jeff Ruetsche, John Pearson, and the rest of the Arcadia Publishing team for helping us on this project.

Photograph credits are abbreviated throughout the text as follows: the Cleveland Press Collection, Cleveland State University Special Collections (CSU), Kent State University Archives (KSU), Greater Akron Baseball Hall of Fame (HOF), and University of Akron Archives (UAA).

INTRODUCTION

From the 1880s through 2006, a list of who's-who and talented hall of famers have graced the local sandlots and stadiums. The list is seemingly endless. The teams in these leagues were considered to be what today would be minor league teams at various levels. Baseball came to the Akron-Canton area in an organized way in 1887. Although statistics and league information were not detailed during those early days, Akron fielded a team named the Akron Acorns. Canton's team was not named. It was not uncommon to have teams known by the area as opposed to having a team nickname. Canton fielded its first team in the league from 1887 to 1888 and 1890. Both the Akron and Canton teams played ball in a league called the Ohio State League. The league fielded nine teams in its initial phase. Throughout its history, the league fielded 23 teams from 1887 to 1890. Teams from as far as Dayton, Michigan, and West Virginia played in the league. In 1889, Canton produced a team called the Canton Nadjys. Akron rejoined the league in 1890 and became known as the Akron Akrons. Not to be left out of the league, Youngstown hit the scene with a team called the Youngstown Giants in 1890. It is also worth noting that in 1890, Denton True Young, or better known as Cy Young, was sold from the Canton team to the Cleveland National League team for $500.

As the Ohio State League disappeared in 1890, another league by the name of the Ohio-Michigan League formed in 1893. The league started with six teams including the Akron Summits and the Canton Deubers. The Deubers disbanded during the season and were replaced with a team from East Liverpool called the East End All Stars. The East End All Stars did not fare much better as they only played in the league for one week.

Baseball teams and leagues would come and go in the area for approximately 40 years until it caught hold in 1928 with the Akron Tyrites. Prior to the Tyrites, Akron had teams known as the Buckeyes (twice, one of which featured Jim Thorpe) who played the minor league Baltimore Orioles. They also had teams named the Rubbernecks, the Champs, the Rubbermen, and the Giants. Barberton had a team called the Barberton Magic Cities. Alliance split a team with Sebring that went by the name of the Twins. Canton had teams named the Watchmakers, the Senators, the Terriors, and the Protectives. The team in Kent was known as the Kings and the Massillon team was known as the Farmers. Youngstown monikers included the Ohio Works, the Champs, the Indians, the Puddlers, and the Steelmen. Most of the above listed teams played in the Ohio-Pennsylvania League. George Sisler was arguably the most talented and famous player from the area to play in this league.

The first real splash of minor league baseball came to Akron in 1935 when it joined the Mid-Atlantic League as a feeder for the New York Yankees. Even though the league faced some difficulties during World War II, the league thrived for over 25 years. The Akron Yankees played in this league until the end of the 1941 season. From 1936 to 1942 the Canton Terriers played in this league as did five teams from Youngstown, the first of which played in 1931. None of the Youngstown teams lasted for more than three consecutive seasons.

The splash of minor league baseball disappeared in the area after the Yankees left Akron. Its resurgence picked up when the Cleveland Indians began bringing in minor league teams closer to home. In 1989, the Burlington, Vermont, team was moved to Canton and became known as the Canton-Akron Indians. They fielded what would become a team of World Series Indians players in the 1990s. With the hit of the new team, other area teams came on the scene. Akron took the team away from Canton in 1997 and renamed the team the Akron Aeros. Akron built a state-of-the-art facility in the downtown area, which many consider to be one of the best minor league parks in the country. The Cleveland Indians sold out 455 consecutive games in the mid- to late 1990s, and it left shut out starving baseball fans screaming for more. The local minor league teams provided an outlet for fans to see quality baseball and development at all levels. In addition to the Aeros, there are the Mahoning Valley Scrappers in Niles and the Lake County Captains in Eastlake. With the loss of the Canton-Akron Indians, the city of Canton brought in an independent team named the Canton Crocodiles of the Frontier League. The team played from 1997 to 2001, and changed its name in 2002 to the Canton Coyotes. The Crocodiles allowed American League Rookie of the Year "Super Joe" Charboneau to bat in 2001, allowing him to bat in professional baseball in four consecutive decades. He of course got a hit.

By having local venues for the big-league team, the Indians have created a euphoric explosion of knowledgeable baseball fans that will last for many years to come. Generation after generation is growing up with awesome stories of the past and dreams of fantastic stories of the future. The local ballparks create what is truly a family atmosphere with intense play on the field from future big-league stars and rehabbing current stars mixed in with fun and games between innings. From fireworks, to mascots, to personal conversations with the players, the Akron-Canton area has become a hotbed for baseball. All summer long, local radio and television stations are filled with baseball talk and clips, with local stars having hopes of playing in the fall classic and making it to "the show." When the locals are not watching, listening, or reading about baseball, they grace the local sandlots and backyards immolating their favorite players. Leagues exist from peewees to seniors and all ages in between. Fantasy league talk buzzes around the water coolers at work. Baseball has influences and has been influenced by such people as Dan Warder, who was inducted into the Greater Akron Baseball Hall of Fame. Not only was he a stellar Double A player in the area, but went on to raise a great family and be a community leader. Baseball truly is the American pastime, and nothing could be closer to the truth in the Akron-Canton area.

1

Major League Professional Baseball Players

It is nearly every child's dream in the United States to one day play in the major leagues. Akron-Canton children's dreams are not that different. However, there is one segment of that dream that is different. The Akron-Canton area can boast having major-leaguers that first played all the way back in the 19th century, long before there were 50 states in the union. Since that time, the level of playing quality has increased significantly. It is not as amazing to hear about a local player making it to the big leagues. It is actually expected. When one thinks about how great many players have been that do not even sniff the fresh grass of a Triple A field, it is truly amazing to imagine how this could be expected. Part of these expectations come from the rich football history of the area, as described in *Akron-Canton Football Heritage*. When residents see local players consistently making it to the NFL, they assume the same for local players making it to the major leagues. However, another part of these expectations comes from the long list of area talent that has made it to the pros. A knowledgeable fan base, with easy access to baseball, compiled with a rich and storied tradition makes what would be unrealistic expectations, very realistic to the people of this area. Much hard work and a little luck have gone into many players being discovered. There truly is an impressive list of local players who have made an impact on major league baseball history. The list includes players such as George Sisler, Thurman Munson, and Gene Michael, just to name a few.

Not only have players touched this area, but many teams have touched this area as well. Major league teams in the early days were not that far from Akron-Canton. Today there is a following of the Yankees from their days of drafting local players to the big leagues. Fans also follow the Reds, the Pirates, and the Blue Jays in addition to their beloved Tribe, often making the trek in the summer to watch them play these other nearby teams. The local newspapers include lists during the summer of how the local heroes are faring in the major and minor leagues. Not enough can be said about the fervor associated with this area and their native sons making the minor leagues and even more can be said about when they make it to "the show."

Bob Addis was born in Mineral, Ohio, in 1925 and attended Barberton High School, where he led the baseball team in every offensive category and earned 12 sports letters. Based on his impressive statistics, Addis was signed as an amateur free agent by the New York Yankees in 1943. His major league career, however, did not start until seven years later (1950) with the Boston Braves, after serving time in the Marine Corps during World War II. Following his stint with the Braves, Addis played for the Chicago Cubs in 1952 and part of 1953, and then finished the year with the Pittsburgh Pirates. He finished his career with a .304 batting average, and his .333 pinch hitting average in 1951 led the National League. In between playing baseball, Addis attended Kent State University, where he obtained his bachelor of arts degree and master of arts degree in education. He retired from baseball following the 1953 season to teach and coach baseball at Euclid High School, winning 402 games and 12 league championships. In 1972, Addis was elected into the Summit County Hall of Fame and in 1995 was inducted into the Greater Akron Baseball Hall of Fame. (HOF.)

Wilmer "Dean" Chance (seen in the photograph on the right after pitching a no-hitter in 1967) was born in Plain Township in 1941 and had a storied pitching career dating back to the Hot Stove Leagues, where he won four championships for West Salem teams. After leading Northwestern High School (in West Salem) to a state championship in 1959 (where he had a four-year record of 51-1), Chance played briefly for the Akron Double A Erhart Kramers before signing with the Baltimore Orioles. He spent two years in their minor league system (1959–1960) before he was selected by the Los Angeles Angels in the expansion draft of 1960. In 1962 (his first full year in the majors), Chance had an impressive 14-10 record and 2.96 ERA and was voted American League Rookie of the Year by the Topps Baseball Card Company. (CSU.)

Dean Chance's most successful season was in 1964, when he compiled a 20-9 win-loss record along with a 1.65 ERA (far right in both photographs). His season was topped off by winning the 1964 Cy Young Award, which at the time was only awarded to one pitcher in major league baseball. At the end of the 1966 season, Chance was traded to the Minnesota Twins, where he spent three seasons (1967–1969). In 1970, he played with both the Cleveland Indians and the New York Mets before retiring at the end of the 1971 season as a member of the Detroit Tigers. His total pitching career included 128 victories, 33 shutouts, two no-hitters, and a 2.92 ERA. Chance was inducted into the Greater Akron Baseball Hall of Fame in 1996. (CSU.)

Dain "Ding-a Ling" Clay was born in Hicksville, Ohio, in 1919. After graduating from Cuyahoga Falls High School, he played for the National Athletic Club team for three years, followed by two years with the Speed Bosworth's Akron Yankees Juniors, a team of all city players. In the two years Clay played with the Yankees Juniors, he batted .400 and was voted the Akron District winner of the Greatest Sandlotter contest by the *Times-Press* in 1937. The following year (1938), Clay signed a contract with the St. Louis Cardinals, but did not play in the major leagues until 1943 with the Cincinnati Reds. He played four years in the major leagues (all with the Cincinnati Reds), compiling a .258 batting average and 98 RBIs. In total, Clay played baseball for 17 years, which included stints with the International, Three I, Texas, Pacific Coast, American Association, Southern, and Western International Leagues. Clay was inducted into the Greater Akron Baseball Hall of Fame in 1993. (HOF.)

Jack DiLauro, born in 1943, started his impressive pitching career in his hometown of Akron as a member of the North Akron Leagues and at North High School. In 1961, he joined the Tramonte Black Labels and in the following year led them to the Double A league championship with an 8-1 pitching record. DiLauro signed as an amateur free agent with the Detroit Tigers in 1962, but he never saw any major league action until he was traded to the New York Mets in December 1968. Although he only pitched one year with the Mets (1969), DiLauro helped the Mets win the 1969 World Series with a 1-4 record and 2.40 ERA. DiLauro spent one more year in the majors (1970) with the Houston Astros, before returning to play local baseball in Akron. As a member of the Eaton Sports Pride in the early 1970s, DiLauro helped the team win two championships and made the all-star team three times. After the 1975 season, DiLauro retired from baseball and became president of the Double A league for two years. DiLauro was inducted into the Greater Akron Baseball Hall of Fame in 1984. (HOF.)

Scott Fletcher was born in 1958 in Fort Walton, Florida, but played youth baseball in Wadsworth (a suburb of Akron). He attended Wadsworth High School (where he was named to the All Ohio baseball team in 1975), and from there played baseball at the University of Toledo and Georgia Southern University. After graduating from college, Fletcher played in the Akron Double A leagues and helped the Acme Ash and Akron Insulating teams win the league championship, as well as receiving the Frank Garcia Award MVP in 1979. He was drafted by the Chicago Cubs as a shortstop in the first round (sixth overall pick) in the 1979 amateur draft, and played with the Cubs from 1981 to 1982. From 1983 to 1985 he played with the Chicago White Sox before being traded to the Texas Rangers in November 1985. Fletcher had his best years with the Rangers, where he is considered to have been their best defensive shortstop, as well as having his highest batting average (.300 in 1986). He rejoined the White Sox from 1989 to 1991, where he had a 56 game errorless streak in 1990. After spending one year with the Milwaukee Brewers in 1992, Fletcher switched to second base and played with the Boston Red Sox from 1993 to 1994 before finishing his career with the Detroit Tigers (1995). Fletcher was inducted into the Greater Akron Baseball Hall of Fame in 1998. (HOF.)

Elmer Flick (far right in photograph, with Harry Bemis and Earl Moore) was born in Bedford in 1876 and lived to be 94. His major league career started in 1898 and finished in 1910. He spent the next two years with Toledo in the minor leagues. He was inducted into the National Baseball Hall of Fame in 1963. "Elmer Flick, the Demon of the Stick" had a lifetime batting average of .313. At the apex of his career, this center fielder was nearly traded even up for Ty Cobb. Cleveland decided to turn the deal down to keep this left-handed hitting, right-handed throwing speedster with a great batting average. Flick led the league in stolen bases two of his 13 years in the major leagues. He also led the league in triples three times. Flick often found himself among the league leaders in walks, which truly shows the fear other teams felt in facing him. He joined the Philadelphia Phillies of the National League to start his career. He jumped ship from the Phillies in an effort to join the cross-town Philadelphia Athletics of the upstart American League. (CSU)

The Phillies were not pleased with Flick's defection to the Athletics (middle in photograph with Luke and Joe Sewell) and had an injunction filed and upheld by the Pennsylvania Supreme Court disallowing him from playing for any team but the Phillies. In an effort to avoid a subpoena, Flick came to Cleveland with fellow teammate Nap Lajoie, who also left the Phillies to join the Athletics. Lajoie once broke his hand in a fistfight with Flick. Eventually the two resolved their differences and Flick ended up playing alongside Lajoie in Cleveland for the Cleveland Broncos. The two players had to travel separately from their team to avoid legal problems in Pennsylvania. The Broncos were soon renamed the Cleveland Naps, after Nap Lajoie. In 1903, the American and National Leagues settled their squabble and both players were again free to enter the state of Pennsylvania. Flick finished his major league career playing for newly named manager Nap Lajoie. The Naps eventually became the Cleveland Indians. (CSU.)

Denny Galehouse was born in Marshallville, Ohio, in 1911 and played youth and semi-professional baseball in nearby Doylestown. He pitched for the Cleveland Indians from 1934 to 1938, followed by a two-year stint with the Boston Red Sox. From 1941 to 1946, Galehouse pitched for the St. Louis Browns, which included a World Series appearance in 1944. During that year, Galehouse primarily pitched on Sundays, while working weekdays at an Akron war plant. In the World Series, he compiled a 1-1 record and a 1.50 ERA, but the Browns ended up losing to the St. Louis Cardinals. Galehouse returned to the Red Sox from 1947 to 1949. His last major league pitching decision was in a 1948 American League playoff game, where the Red Sox lost 8-3 to the Cleveland Indians. Galehouse was inducted into the Greater Akron Baseball Hall of Fame in 1987. (HOF.)

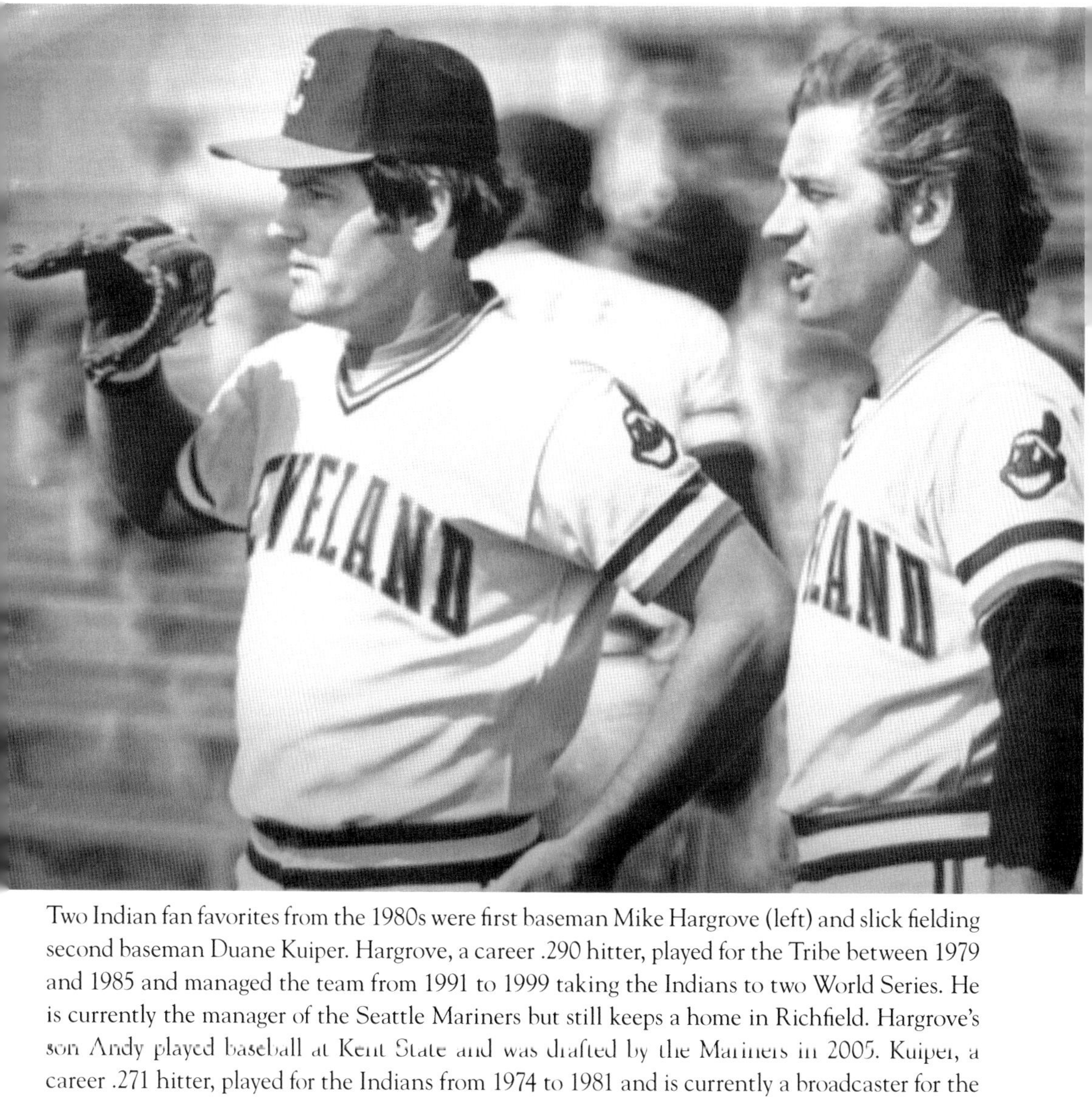

Two Indian fan favorites from the 1980s were first baseman Mike Hargrove (left) and slick fielding second baseman Duane Kuiper. Hargrove, a career .290 hitter, played for the Tribe between 1979 and 1985 and managed the team from 1991 to 1999 taking the Indians to two World Series. He is currently the manager of the Seattle Mariners but still keeps a home in Richfield. Hargrove's son Andy played baseball at Kent State and was drafted by the Mariners in 2005. Kuiper, a career .271 hitter, played for the Indians from 1974 to 1981 and is currently a broadcaster for the San Francisco Giants. (CSU)

Charles Hostetler was born in McClellandtown, Pennsylvania, in 1903, but was raised in Ravenna, Ohio. He made a name for himself playing for the General Tire Team of Akron in 1925 and the Akron Tyrites of the Central League in 1927. After spending some time playing baseball in Tulsa, Oklahoma, and Topeka, Kansas, Hostetler finally made it to the big leagues with the Detroit Tigers in 1944 at the ripe old age of 41. He played 98 games with the Tigers that year, batting .298 with 20 RBIs. The following year, Hostetler was used primarily as a pinch hitter, but nevertheless helped the Tigers win the 1945 World Series against the Chicago Cubs. He was released from the Tigers in January 1946. Hostetler was the first inductee of the Greater Akron Baseball Hall of Fame (class of 1996) that played baseball in the early 1920s. (HOF.)

Art "Cave" Kusnyer was born in Akron in 1945. He was a catcher for numerous West Akron Baseball League (WABL) championship teams, such as the champion Akron Blues, the Class D champion Trainer Sports, and Buchtel High School. Kusnyer's amateur career (primarily Double A baseball) included stints with the Tiny's Orphans, Triner Sports, Joe's All-Stars, and the 1966 Double A champion Airmatic Valve. He won the Frank Garcia outstanding player award for Double A ball in 1965, and hit over .400 during that time. In 1966, Kusnyer was drafted by the Chicago White Sox and played his first major league game with the team in 1970. He also played for the California Angels (1971–1973), Milwaukee Brewers (1976), and Kansas City Royals (1978). With the Angels, Kusnyer had the distinction of catching one of Nolan Ryan's no-hitters (1973). After retiring from baseball, Kusnyer turned his focus to coaching. Currently he is enjoying his second stint as bullpen coach for the Chicago White Sox (ninth season). Kusnyer was inducted into the Greater Akron Baseball Hall of Fame in 1986. (HOF.)

John Anthony "Tony" Mullane was born in Cork, Ireland, in 1859 and immigrated to the United States when he was five years old. Originally a right-handed pitcher, Mullane taught himself how to pitch left-handed when he suffered an injury to his right arm. After the arm healed, he continued to pitch with both arms, putting both hands on the ball and then choosing one or the other to pitch. Mullane first pitched for the 1880–1881 Akron Independents, which was considered the best independent team in the country at that time. He first saw major league action in August 1881 with the Detroit Wolverines of the National League. Mullane played from 1882 to 1884 in both the American Association and the National League. During his 13-year career, he compiled a record of 284-220 with a 3.05 ERA, had five 30-win seasons (1882–1884; 1886–1887), and pitched one no-hitter (September 11, 1882). Mullane was inducted into the Greater Akron Baseball Hall of Fame in 2003. (HOF.)

Hal Naragon (catcher in both photographs) was born in Zanesville, Ohio, in 1928, but started his playing career in the Barberton Youth Leagues and at Barberton High School. After high school, Naragon played catcher for the Kenmore Tavern and the Akron Orphans before being signed by the Cleveland Indians in 1947. He played with the Indians in 1951. His career was interrupted by military service during the 1952 and 1953 seasons. Naragon rejoined the Indians from 1954 to 1959, playing with the team in the 1954 World Series. Naragon then played for the Washington Senators from 1959 to 1960, followed by two years with the Minnesota Twins before retiring. Overall, Naragon had a .266 batting average with six home runs and 87 RBIs. (CSU.)

After his retirement, Hal Naragon (behind Henry Aguirre in top photograph, applying the tag at home plate in bottom photograph) coached for the Detroit Tigers and Minnesota Twins in the 1960s, but then changed his focus to youth baseball, specifically around the Barberton area. Based on his commitment to youth sports, approachability, and kindness, Barberton High School renamed its sports complex Hal Naragon Field in April 2006. Naragon was inducted into the Greater Akron Baseball Hall of Fame in 1991. (CSU.)

Ron "Do-It" Pruitt (seen here being congratulated by teammate Duane Kuiper in a 1978 game) was born in Flint, Michigan, but makes his home in Medina. He is currently running the Ron Pruitt Baseball Center in Medina. Pruitt had quite a career as a catcher. He graduated from Michigan State University with the distinction of being an All–Big Ten catcher in 1971 and 1972, as well as an All-American catcher in 1972. He was a second round pick of the Texas Rangers and became an all-star catcher three times as he worked his way through the minor leagues. In 1975, he was given the chance to catch his first big-league game. The pitcher was no less than Gaylord Perry. Pruitt was soon traded from the Rangers to the Cleveland Indians where he spent most of his major league baseball career. (CSU.)

After his time in Cleveland, Ron Pruitt (seen at far left in the photograph, taken in 1978 with Fred Kendall and Ron Hassey) was traded to the Chicago White Sox, then came back to the Indians for a brief stint before finishing his big-league career with the San Francisco Giants. Pruitt had some exciting plays during his baseball career. He hit a home run at old Cleveland Municipal Stadium on opening day, caught a number of hall of fame pitchers, and played alongside American League Rookie of the Year Joe Charboneau as well as perfect-game-pitcher Lenny Barker. His talents did not limit him to sitting behind the dish. On occasion, he could be found in the outfield and both corners of the diamond. Pruitt once owned a video store in the Montrose area and is a very approachable family man. (CSU.)

Luke Sewell, pictured far left in 1944 with future baseball commissioner Happy Chandler (in suit and hat), played major league baseball for 20 years. A majority of that time, 1921 to 1932 and 1939, was spent playing for the Indians. Sewell finished his career a .259 hitter and was known as a fine defensive catcher. Although originally from Alabama, Sewell settled in the area and passed away in Akron in 1987. He was one of three brothers to have played major league baseball along with Tommy and Joe, a hall of famer who also spent a significant portion of his career with the Indians. (CSU.)

This collection of Indians greats includes Akron's Luke Sewell (seen here in the middle). Others included are hall of famers Bob Lemon and Luke's brother Joe (to the left of Luke) along with power hitting first basemen Hal Trosky and Vic Wertz. Trosky played for the Tribe between 1933 and 1941, belting out 228 home runs to go along with a .302 average. Wertz played for the Indians between 1954 and 1958 and had 266 career home runs. (CSU)

Another all-time great with local ties was Lefty Grove. Grove, pictured at the right with Cy Young, went 300-141 between 1925 and 1941, splitting time between the Philadelphia Athletics and the Boston Red Sox. After his career he settled in the area and died in Norwalk in 1975. He was elected to the National Baseball Hall of Fame in 1947. (CSU.)

In his day, Herb Score (right) was one of the best pitchers in the major leagues. During his first two seasons he went 36-19 with 508 strikeouts for the Indians between 1955 and 1956. He was seriously injured during the 1957 season and was never quite the same. Fortunately for northeast Ohio, Score got involved in broadcasting and is more famous now for his time in the booth than on the field. He worked Indians television games between 1964 and 1967, and then switched to radio where he was the voice of Indians baseball from 1968 to 1997. Score is pictured here during spring training in 1956 with catcher Jim Hegan. Hegan was the Tribe's catcher from 1941 to 1957, working behind the plate for numerous hall of fame pitchers including Bob Feller and Bob Lemon. Interestingly enough, Hegan's son Mike, who was born in Cleveland in 1942 and played major league baseball for 12 seasons, has been broadcasting for the Indians since 1989. (CSU.)

George Sisler was born in Manchester (a suburb of Akron) in 1893. He played for Central High School and Barberton Babcock and Wilcox Company before attending the University of Michigan. Sisler signed as a free agent with the St. Louis Browns in 1915 as a pitcher, but switched to first base the following year due to the strength of his bat. His best years were 1920 and 1922, when he had a batting average of .407 and .420 respectively, thus making him one of only three players to hit above .400 twice in a career. Furthermore, in 1922, on the strength of his batting average (third highest in the 20th century) and a 41 game hitting streak, Sisler was awarded the inaugural Most Valuable Player (MVP) in the American League. He missed the entire 1923 season due to sinusitis, but returned to the Browns for another four years. In 1928, the Browns sold his contract to the Washington Senators, who in turn sold his rights to the Boston Braves. Sisler ended his professional career with the Braves following the 1930 season. In his 15 years in the majors, Sisler had a career batting average of .340, only hitting below .300 in two seasons. Sisler was elected to the National Baseball Hall of Fame in 1939, the Summit County Sports Hall of Fame in 1957, and the Greater Akron Baseball Hall of Fame in 1983. (HOF.)

Two all-time greats with local ties are pictured here well after their playing days have ended. Tris Speaker (right) was elected to the National Baseball Hall of Fame in 1937 after accumulating 3,515 hits (including a record 793 doubles) and a .344 lifetime average. He played for the Indians from 1916 to 1926 and led them to a World Series title in 1920. Cy Young (left) finished his pitching career with a record mark of 511-313 and was also elected to the hall of fame in 1937. He was born in Gilmore in 1867 and passed away in Peoli in 1955. He pitched for the old National League Cleveland franchise from 1890 to 1898, and for the American League club from 1909 to 1911. (CSU.)

Jeff Tabaka was born in Barberton in 1964, but grew up in nearby Copley. At Copley High School, he was elected all-suburban league and all-district for both his pitching and hitting abilities. Tabaka then attended Kent State University, where he earned four varsity K letters in baseball from 1983 to 1986. As a pitcher at Kent State University, Tabaka set records for saves in a season with eight, and had a four-year record of 10-6 with 79 strikeouts. At the same time, he batted .350 and had 14 home runs with 84 RBIs. Immediately after college, Tabaka was drafted in the second round by the Montreal Expos in the 1986 baseball draft. He played in his first major league game in 1994 with the Pittsburgh Pirates. Overall Tabaka played for five major league teams—Pittsburgh Pirates (twice), San Diego Padres, Houston Astros, Cincinnati Reds, and St. Louis Cardinals—before retiring from baseball after the 2001 season. An interesting note in his career is that he was the last player drafted in the expansion draft by the Florida Marlins in 1992. Tabaka was elected into the Kent State Athletic Hall of Fame in 1998 and the Greater Akron Baseball Hall of Fame in 2003.

Jacubus Franciscus Thorpe, better known as Jim Thorpe, was best known for playing football and being in the Olympics. However, he was a multi-talented athlete who was very good at playing baseball and basketball as well. Thorpe was born on May 28, 1887, in Prague, Oklahoma. Thorpe's Native American name was Wa-Tho-Huk, which means "Bright Path." While playing football for the Canton Bulldogs, Thorpe found time to play baseball as well. He played baseball for the Akron Buckeyes. His major league days saw him playing for the New York Giants, the Cincinnati Reds, and the Boston Braves. Although he traveled around the world, Canton has always counted him as one of its own. There has arguably never been a better overall athlete ever born. He participated in the 1917 World Series and finished his career in the minor leagues. As a baseball player, he mostly roamed the outfield, but could be seen at first base a few times. He was stripped of his Olympic medals because he was considered to be a professional athlete. His Olympic medals came from track and field (which is obviously unrelated to football, baseball, and basketball where he received compensation). He was eventually awarded the medals he earned and deserved from the Olympic Committee posthumously. Thorpe was famous all around the world and chose to spend most of his time playing football in Ohio while keeping his baseball skills sharp. (CSU.)

Eugene "Gene" Woodling (left in the photograph, greeting teammate Ray Mack and family) was born in 1922 in Akron where he spent his youth playing in East Akron youth leagues and East High School. He signed as a free agent with the Cleveland Indians as an outfielder in 1940, but spent the first four years with the Indians in the minor leagues. During this time, Woodling won four minor league batting titles, starting in Mansfield. He played just eight games with the Indians in 1943 before serving in the U.S. Navy from 1944 to 1945. He returned to the Indians in 1946 for 61 games, and the following year played 24 games with the Pittsburgh Pirates. (CSU.)

After the 1948 season, Woodling's contract was purchased by the New York Yankees from the San Francisco Seals. Woodling spent six years with the Yankees, where he played in five consecutive World Series championships (1949–1953). During that stretch, he hit .318 and was selected World Series MVP three times. At the end of the 1954 season, Woodling was traded to the Baltimore Orioles in a record 17 player deal. He is seen in the first row, on the far right of the photograph. (CSU.)

In the next several years, Woodling played for the Cleveland Indians (1955–1957), Baltimore Orioles (1958–1960), and Washington Senators (1961). Woodling finished his career with the New York Mets in 1962. After his retirement, Woodling continued to influence baseball by helping to establish a pension fund for ballplayers. He is on the left of the photograph with manager Al Lopez. Woodling was inducted into the Greater Akron Baseball Hall of Fame in 1989. (CSU.)

At the end of his 17-year baseball career, Gene Woodling had a career batting average of .284, with 147 home runs and 830 RBIs. His productive offensive numbers were helped by his hustle on the bases, as seen in these photographs from 1950 and 1957 respectively. (CSU.)

2

Minor League Baseball

Every ballplayer's goal is to make it to the major leagues. However, something can be said for a career in the minors. Today minor league baseball is light-years ahead of where it used to be in its early days. Not only is travel better, but there is a deeply rooted fan base that turns otherwise unknown people into local heroes. The major league teams have put their minor league affiliates closer to home, constantly evaluating and reevaluating each player's development. Training methods and instruction have tremendously improved. It is not easy to hide in the minors when one is not producing. The level of talent has exploded at the minor league level. Fans are treated to seeing superstars rehab at local minor league parks since they are so close to the major league parent club. It is still a treat to take the family to minor league games, where the atmosphere is relaxed while still seeing a quality product on the field. Occasionally one may hear advice from a coach to a player during a game. Sitting virtually on the field is another benefit fans have come to appreciate. Minor league facilities really provide an intimate relationship between the fans and the team that is not seen elsewhere.

Minor league baseball has come and gone in this area on numerous occasions over the last century or so. This time, minor league baseball has come to stay. It can be seen in its early forms from local sandlots to its modern forms with state-of-the-art ballparks. A large factor behind this has to do with the Cleveland Indians. The Indians of late have enjoyed some of the largest attendance marks both in major league and minor league history. During the Indians return to the World Series in the 1990s, they realized that they had more fans than seats. The fans were clamoring for more. That fan base was in their own backyard, with the exception of the Buffalo Bisons who are not that far away. The Indians realized that a large baseball fan base grew up with the Akron-Canton Indians in the late 1980s and early 1990s. Many of those players made it through the farm system to the Tribe and eventually played in the World Series. The fans really felt a special bond with these players and the Indians. Soon more teams came to the area and have enjoyed great success.

Former University of Akron football coach and current Walsh University head football coach Jim Dennison started his athletic career on the diamond at both Wadsworth High School and the College of Wooster as a second baseman and outfielder. After graduation, Dennison became the player-manager of the Wadsworth Merchants, leading them to the Tri-County League title in 1960. From 1960 to 1964, Dennison coached baseball at Wadsworth and Elyria High School as well as playing baseball for Lorain Wolf Dry Goods and the Elyria Mustangs in the Lakewood League. He also played for Akron teams such as Krispy Kremes, P.O.C. Beer, Airmatic Valve, Weather Seal, and the Red Peppers (where he was both player and manager from 1970 to 1972). During this 17-year span (including his four-year college career), Dennison had a career batting average above .300 in 14 seasons, and was an all-star in all three leagues he played. In 1973, Dennison left baseball behind to become the head football coach of the University of Akron, where he led them to a record of 80-62-2 between 1973 and 1985, making him the winningest coach in university history. Dennison was inducted into the Greater Akron Baseball Hall of Fame in 1986. (UAA.)

Although known primarily as a football coach, Massillon native Ara Parseghian (third from left) was a talented baseball player in his youth. He played first base and was a pitcher for the National Athletic Club team in his teens, advancing to the championship Grays IGA team of the American Legion. At the age of 17, Parseghian was elected to the first Akron Orphan team of high school all-stars. He remained with the Akron Orphans until he enlisted in the U.S. Navy in 1943. Parseghian continued to play some baseball during his time in the U.S. Navy, and even had a tryout with the Pittsburgh Pirates arranged following his discharge. However, he instead decided to enroll at Miami University of Ohio and focus on football. After a brief football career with the Cleveland Browns (1947 to 1948), Parseghian turned his attention to coaching, where he was most successful as the head football coach of Notre Dame, leading them to a 95-17-4 record and two national championships from 1964 to 1974. Parseghian was inducted into the Greater Akron Baseball Hall of Fame in 1994. (CSU.)

The Akron Aeros are an affiliate of the Cleveland Indians in the Double A Eastern League. The team was founded by Mike Agganis in 1980 and began playing in Lynn, Massachusetts, as the Lynn Sailors. In 1984, Agganis moved the team to Burlington, Vermont, and they became the affiliate of the Cincinnati Reds (renamed the Vermont Reds). After four years in Vermont (the first three as the Vermont Reds, and the last year as the Vermont Mariners), Agganis moved the team once again in 1989 to Canton and they became the new Double A Cleveland Indians affiliate. Renamed the Canton-Akron Indians, the team played their home games at Thurman Munson Memorial Stadium from 1989 to 1996. During that span, the team made the playoffs in five straight seasons (1989–1993), but never managed to win a league championship.

In the fall of 1994, Mike Agganis signed a lease to move the Canton-Akron Indians to downtown Akron. The team played in Canton for two more years before finally moving to Akron in 1997. With the move came a name change to the franchise: the Akron Aeros. The name was chosen to honor the history of aerospace in Ohio (which includes being the home state of the Wright Brothers, Neil Armstrong, and John Glenn). The Aeros name beat out two other choices: Spirit and Quest. For their first three seasons in Akron, the Aeros had the highest total attendance for any Double A baseball team. The team has made the playoffs in 5 out of the 10 years they have been in Akron (1997–2006), wining the league championship in 2003 and 2005.

Canal Park, located in downtown Akron, has been the home of the Akron Aeros since 1997. The park was designed by Hellmuth, Obata and Kassabaum, which also designed, among other parks, Jacobs Field (home of the Cleveland Indians) and Oriole Park at Camden Yards (home of the Baltimore Orioles). Groundbreaking was held on January 5, 1996, and construction was finished on January 31, 1997, at a cost of $31 million. The Aeros played their first game at Canal Park on April 10, 1997, against the Harrisburg Senators in front of 9,086 fans.

Part of Canal Park's architecture is a replica of the clock tower at the Goodyear Tire and Rubber Company. The company, which is the third largest tire and rubber manufacturing company in the world, helped earn Akron the nickname "the Rubber City."

Canal Park's scoreboard is the largest free-standing one in the minor leagues (56 feet 3 inches by 68 feet). It also has full color animation capacity with a four color matrix display.

The Akron Aeros celebrated their 10th year at Canal Park in 2006. To celebrate this milestone, fans were given this commemorative poster on August 16, 2006. As seen in the poster, many major league baseball players have played, at some point in their careers, for the Aeros. Some notable former players include Albert Belle, Manny Ramirez, Grady Sizemore, Jim Thome, Victor Martinez, and C. C. Sabathia.

Canal Park seats a total of 9,097, with capacity increasing to 12,500 when seats are included on the field. There are also 25 luxury suites, as well as a press box located above home plate. The field dimensions are: left field 331 feet, left-center field 376 feet, center field 400 feet; right-center field 375 feet; and right field 337 feet. When sitting on the third-base line, a clear view of downtown Akron is possible.

Along the third-base sideline of Canal Park sits the Aero's clubhouse. Spanning more than 9,000 square feet, the clubhouse includes two batting and pitching cages, a workout facility, a training room, a player's lounge, and the manager's and coaches offices. The visitor clubhouse is equally impressive, with 6,000 square feet of space that includes a training room, offices for the visiting manager and coaches, as well as 30 lockers for the players.

To block the sun from the batter's eyes, a wall was constructed along the right-center line, thus drawing comparisons to the Green Monster wall at Fenway Park, home of the Boston Red Sox.

Orbit, the Akron Aeros mascot, is a favorite of fans of all ages. He can be seen during the game signing autographs and participating in events such as leading fans in sing-a-longs and running the bases with children. He is also the "president" of both Orbit's Baseball Buddies and Silver Sluggers, clubs that offer special giveaways and activities for children under 12 years and seniors older than 60.

It used to be all one could get was a hot dog, beer, pop, and crackerjacks at a ball game. Today food is just as much a part of the game as the game itself. Menches Brother's, "inventors of the original hamburger," is located above right field in Canal Park, allowing fans to enjoy a relaxing and filling meal along with the game. Also along the right field line is Infield Outfitters, the Aeros' merchandise shop, which is unique in the sense that it is open all year long.

Regardless of where one sits at Canal Park, every seat is a good one. When the Aeros are batting, one can see all of the infield action from the motion of the pitcher to the swing of the bat (as seen in the above picture featuring Aeros' right fielder Brad Snyder). Or for a different perspective, one can focus on a single motion, like the batter charging to first base (as seen in the picture below featuring Aeros' third baseman Pat Osborn).

Defensive gems can be seen quite clearly at Canal Park. In these pictures, Aeros' second baseman Shaun Larkin and first baseman Ryan Mulhern are set and waiting for the pitch. Once the pitch is hit, shortstop Ivan Ochoa and Mulhern combine for a sweet double play. Unfortunately, their effort was not good enough, as the Aeros went on to lose the game to the Reading Phillies by a score of 6-1.

Year	Record	Place in Division
1989	70-69	3rd
1990	76-64	3rd
1991	75-65	4th
1992	80-58	1st
1993	75-63	2nd
1994	67-73	6th
1995	67-75	5th
1996	71-71	3rd
1997	51-90	5th
1998	81-60	1st
1999	69-71	5th
2000	75-68	3rd
2001	68-74	3rd
2002	93-48	1st
2003	88-53	1st
2004	63-78	5th
2005	84-58	1st
2006	87-55	1st

This is the Akron Aeros record from 1989 to 2006. Note that from 1989 to 1996, the team was named the Canton-Akron Indians. In 2003 and 2005 the Akron Aeros were the Eastern League champions.

Year	Description
1989	Lost in first round to Harrisburg (3-2)
1990	Lost in first round to London (3-2)
1991	Lost in first round to Harrisburg (3-1)
1992	Defeated Albany-Colonie in first round (3-1); lost in league championship series to Binghamton (3-2)
1993	Defeated Bowie in first round (3-2); lost in league championship series to Harrisburg (3-2)
1998	Lost in first round to Harrisburg (3-1)
2002	Lost in first round to Harrisburg (3-2)
2003	Defeated Altoona in first round (3-1); won league championship over New Haven (3-0)
2005	Defeated Altoona in first round (3-2); won league championship over Portland (3-1)
2006	Defeated Altoona in first round (3-2); lost league championship to Portland (3-2)

This is the Akron Aeros playoff description.

The Lake County Captains are a baseball team affiliated with the Cleveland Indians in the Single A South Atlantic League. The Captains were originally the Columbus RedStixx (from Georgia) before being moved to northeast Ohio after the 2002 season by owners Peter A. Carfagna and Rita Murphy-Carfagna, both born and raised in Cleveland. Total game attendance has surpassed 1.2 million in the three years the Captains have been in Ohio.

In their inaugural season in northeast Ohio, the Captains had their most successful season in their franchise history, posting a 97-43 record. Under manager Luis Rivera, the team made it to the finals of the South Atlantic League playoffs, where they lost to the Rome Braves, three games to one. In 2004, the Captains posted a record of 73-66 (fifth best in the league), but finished out of the playoff picture. In 2005, the Captains had a nearly identical record as that of 2004 (72-66), but again failed to make the playoffs. The following year (2006), the Captains finished the season below .500 for the first time since moving to Ohio (64-74).

The Lake County Captains play their home games at Classic Park, located in Eastlake. Built for approximately $20 million by Turner Construction and designed by DLR Group, the stadium was originally called Eastlake Stadium before the team sold the naming rights to Classic Automotive Group in 2005. The stadium includes a 4,000 square foot indoor batting complex with two batting cages. The Captains played their first game at the new stadium on April 10, 2003, to a near sell-out crowd (7,124). In 2006, the stadium hosted the South Atlantic League All-Star Game.

The playing field at Classic Park was voted Best Playing Surface in the South Atlantic League in 2003 and 2004. Behind the right field fence is the main clubhouse for both the Captains and the visiting teams. The clubhouse has a training room, offices for the manager and coaching staff, and laundry facilities.

Classic Park has 7,273 seats and 20 luxury suites (above). Behind home plate in the upper deck is the press box, where radio stations WELW (1330 AM) and WTAM (850 AM) broadcast the exciting action. Seating is also available along the outfield wall (below) as well as standing room behind the seats, increasing the stadium capacity to above 10,000. Sitting behind center and left field is the scoreboard, which broadcasts action from the game and in the stands.

Classic Park also has two designated picnic areas, allowing fans of all ages to enjoy a bite to eat before or during the game.

This pedestrian walkway not only links Classic Park to the adjacent parking lot, but also provides passing cars information on their favorite minor league team.

On the wall of Classic Park, one can see the starting lineups of the Lake County Captains and visitors, as well as the standings in the Atlantic South League. On this date (June 4, 2006), the Captains played the West Virginia Power, a Milwaukee Brewers affiliate.

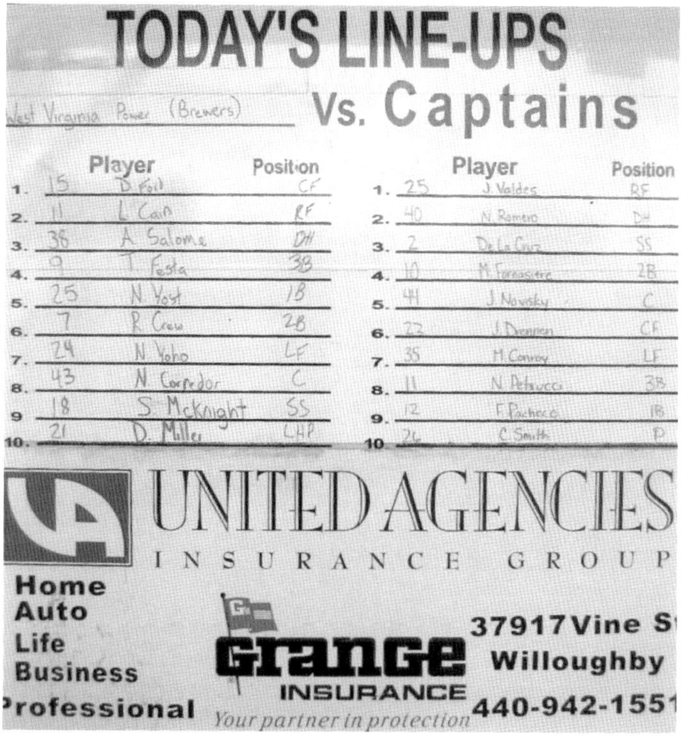

Along the right field line sits the Lake County Captains' bullpen. Anyone can look over the fence and see players warming up and talking among themselves. The above photograph shows Captains' pitcher Carlton Smith getting ready for a game against the West Virginia Power on June 4, 2006. Smith at the time had a record of 1-2 with an ERA of 4.85.

Classic Park allows fans to see the action up close without any obstruction. One can even hear the crack of the bat when the batter makes contact with the ball. Shown here are third baseman Nick Petrucci (above) and right fielder Juan Valdes (below) at bat against the West Virginia Power. Petrucci was batting .201 with two home runs and 12 RBIs, while Valdes, who might only be a "cup of coffee" away from being called up to the big leagues, was batting .229 with two home runs and 13 RBIs.

Another advantage of seeing the Lake County Captains play is that one can see great defensive plays up close. In the above photograph, second baseman Matt Fornasiere makes a leaping throw to first base after getting the force out at second base on Ryan Crew of the West Virginia Power. Fornasiere has the distinction of being one of three players to get a hit off of pitcher Roger Clemens when he pitched three innings for the Lexington Legends as a tune-up for returning to the majors (June 6, 2006). In the photograph below, first basemen Fernando Pacheco steps on first base, forcing out West Virginia player Nestor Corredor.

What would a baseball game be like without seeing a manager argue with the umpire? Seen in this photograph is first-year Lake County Captain manager Lee May Jr. (No. 30, son of major league player Lee May Sr.) arguing with the umpire when a West Virginia Power player was called safe at third base. West Virginia went on to win the game 7-3, despite the Captains outhitting the Power 13 12.

Seen in these photographs is Lake County Captains' catcher/designated hitter Max Ramirez batting against the Lakewood BlueClaws in August 2006. Ramirez is of note since he was obtained from the Atlanta Braves in 2006 for Cleveland Indians all-time save record-holder Bob Wickman. Hopefully in a couple of years he will have Indians fans asking "Bob who?" So far, Ramirez is off to a promising start. In only 37 games with the Captains, Ramirez batted .307 with four home runs and 26 RBIs.

In a June 2006 game, fans were able to see Ned Yost pass through the area as a first baseman of the West Virginia Power playing against the Captains at Canal Park. Not only does having local minor league teams in the area provide local talented players, but it also brings in talent from around the country. This makes for great entertainment. Ned is the son of former major league player and current major league manager of the Milwaukee Brewers Ned Yost. Father Ned had the opportunity to play in the World Series for the St. Louis Cardinals and was a backup catcher for the Milwaukee Brewers during his career. Son Ned hopes to follow in his father's footsteps by playing in the major leagues some day soon. He does not appear to be too far away.

Skipper, the team mascot of the Lake County Captains, made his first appearance at the opening day of Classic Park (April 10, 2003) and has been with the team ever since. One can find him before, during, and after games entertaining fans of all ages, from tossing T-shirts into the crowd, to leading fans in cheering contests, to dancing on top of the dugout. He can even be seen on the playing field calling balls and strikes during pregame activities (below).

The Mahoning Valley Scrappers are a minor league baseball team in the Single A New York–Penn League. Originally known as the Erie SeaWolves, the team moved to Ohio in 1999 to make room for a Double A team affiliated with the Anaheim Angels. The Scrappers, an affiliate of the Cleveland Indians, play ball from the end of June (after professional teams have signed their draft picks) to the early part of September.

Since joining the New York–Penn League in 1999, the Scrappers have won two division titles: McNamara Division in 1999, and the Pinckney Division in 2000. In both of those years, the Scrappers lost in the championship round of the playoffs (to the Hudson Valley Renegades in 1999 and to the Staten Island Yankees in 2000). In 2004, the Scrappers placed second in their division (Pinckney), yet went on to win the league championship by defeating the Tri-City Valley Cats two games to zero.

Many major league players started their professional career with the Mahoning Valley Scrappers. Shown here are street flags celebrating two players who not only played with the Scrappers, but presently (2006) play professional ball with the neighboring Cleveland Indians: C. C. Sabathia and Victor Martinez. Sabathia played only one month with the Scrappers in 1999 before being promoted to the Columbus RedStixx (Georgia), while Martinez played all of 1999 with the Scrappers before being promoted to the Akron Aeros the following year. Other famous alumni include Josh Bard, Ryan Garko, Brian Tallet, Einar Diaz, John McDonald, Mike Edwards, Marshall McDougal, and Lou Merloni.

The Mahoning Valley Scrappers play their home games at Eastwood Field (above), located in Niles (approximately halfway between Cleveland and Pittsburgh). The stadium was built in 1999 and was originally called Cafaro Field after William M. Cafaro, founder of Cafaro Company (below). In 2003, the name of the stadium was changed to Eastwood Field in order to match the name of another Cafaro Company property, Eastwood Mall (which the stadium is located behind). The stadium has 6,000 seats, natural grass, and stadium lighting. Attendance for Scrapper's games averages over 4,000 per game.

Besides being the home of the Scrappers, Eastwood Field is also the home of the Youngstown State University baseball team, as well as hosting spring and summer concerts (where the seating capacity increases to 10,000), and other sporting events. For example, in May 2006, Eastwood Field hosted the National Club Baseball Association World Series. The National Club Baseball Association allows college students to continue to play competitive baseball and is unique in the sense that the entire organization (from equipment purchases to travel arrangements to scheduling) is run by the students themselves. The game seen in this photograph is No. 1 seed Penn State University (batting) versus No. 5 seed University of Texas (pitching).

3

Local Colleges and Universities

Unlike the major leagues, minor league baseball and college baseball have constant turnover. It is difficult to build a core team and even more difficult to build a team in the north, where there are fewer playing days because of the weather. Unlike football, many baseball players, upon graduating high school, decide to go straight to the minor and major leagues (via way of rookie ball) as opposed to playing ball in college. Yet the local colleges and universities have not let that stop them. They have been able to field competitive teams that send players to the major leagues.

The University of Akron is headed by Pat Bangston and plays its home games at Lee Jackson Field. Lee Jackson Field holds a capacity crowd of 1,500 people. The enrollment is nearly 23,000. The Zips last won the Mid-American Conference (MAC) baseball tournament in 1996. They have also been competitive in softball, starting a team in the 1976–1977 season, and they eventually won the MAC regular season in 1998.

Like the Zips, the Kent State Golden Flashes play in the MAC. Kent's enrollment is approximately 33,000 students. Kent State leads the local collegiate area in sending players to the big leagues. The Kent baseball class of 2006 was rated 17th in the country. The Kent State Baseball program has been in existence since 1915 and plays its home games at Shoonover Stadium. Six players made it to the majors who did not play on the team, but attended the school. However, there is a long list of players who have. Kent also has a competitive women's softball team.

Malone College has just over 2,300 students and first fielded a baseball team in 1963. The Malone Pioneers have established themselves quite a history under head coach Bob Starcher. During his 23 years leading the Pioneers, they enjoyed 19 winning seasons and 12 titles. Former major league and University of Akron standout John Massarelli, who was named the 2004 and 2006 Manager of the Year in the Frontier League with the Washington Wild Things, has been assisting the Malone baseball team in an effort to continue their winning tradition. Heading into the 2007 season, Malone is ranked 33rd in the nation in the National Association of Intercollegiate Athletics. Walsh University and the College of Wooster have also been competitive in local collegiate baseball, keeping the spirit alive and well in the area.

The University of Akron was formally known as Buchtel College from 1870 to 1913. Shown here is the 1911 Buchtel College baseball squad on the first day of practice. Captain Cassius Sisler and manager Frank McMillen led the team to a 4-3 mark competing against the likes of Kenyon, Mount Union, and Oberlin Colleges. In a no-lose situation for the fans, the team finished up playing an alumni team. (UAA.)

The 1925 University of Akron baseball team featured Levi MacDonald as the captain and Clyde Tiley as the manager. The squad, which finished the year 2-5, had the unfortunate distinction of not playing any home games due to their field being regraded. They were able to finish up the campaign on a high note, beating Mount Union 8-0 in the finale. (UAA.)

The 1965 University of Akron baseball team finished 14-8 (10-5 in the Ohio conference) behind its stellar pitching staff. Jim Barton (second row, far left) led the conference with 112 strikeouts and Ray Glinsky (first row, third from left) finished his career with a 20-6 mark. (UAA.)

The 1981 Zips squad finished with a 23-17-2 mark and featured two players who would excel in sports after their collegiate playing days were over. Mike Birkbeck (first row, second from left) would go on to pitch in the major leagues while teammate Keith Dambrot (first row, second from right) would switch gears and become a very successful basketball coach. (UAA.)

Keith Dambrot, shown here in a 1980 game at shortstop, graduated from the University of Akron in 1982. He was a three-year starter and team captain while playing baseball for the Zips, but has since switched his interest to coaching basketball. From 1998 to 2001, Dambrot was the head basketball coach at St. Vincent–St. Mary High School in Akron. He won a couple of state championships along the way, with a little help from a player named Lebron James. Dambrot took over the head coaching job for the University of Akron's basketball team in March 2004. The team's 23-10 mark in 2005–2006 is evidence of Dambrot's leadership ability on the court. (UAA.)

All-American
Mike Birkbeck

Mike Birkbeck was born in 1961 in Orrville. He was an All-Ohio Conference All-Star three times in high school and led the Orrville High Red Riders to the league title in 1979. Birkbeck played baseball for the University of Akron from 1980 to 1983. He compiled a win-loss record of 24-9 with the Zips, while batting .367 with 25 home runs and 117 RBIs. Birkbeck was also captain of the Zip's baseball team in 1982–1983, All-Ohio Valley Conference in 1982–1983, and was Zip Player of the Year and an All-American in 1982. After graduating, Birkbeck was drafted as a pitcher in the fourth round of the 1983 baseball draft by the Milwaukee Brewers. He played for the Brewers from 1986 to 1990, appearing in 54 games and compiling a 12-19 record and 4.86 ERA. After being released by the Brewers at the end of the 1990 season, Birkbeck next played at the major league level with the New York Mets in 1992 and again in 1995. He was released by the Mets in June 1995, he then played in Japan the rest of the year and part of 1996 until a broken leg forced him to retire in September 1996. Birkbeck is currently entering his 11th year as pitching coach of the Kent State University baseball team. He was elected to the University of Akron Varsity A Hall of Fame in 1992 and the Greater Akron Baseball Hall of Fame in 2001. (UAA.)

One of the more successful teams of the last 20 years at the University of Akron was the 1987 squad. The team finished with an overall mark of 34-19 (13-6 in the Ohio Valley Conference) and just missed out on a trip to the NCAA tournament, losing 9-8 to Middle Tennessee State University in the Ohio Valley Conference championship game. (UAA)

The star of that 1987 team was Massillon resident John Massarelli. Massarelli batted .419 that season with 50 RBIs. Shortly after the season ended, he was drafted in the eighth round of the major league draft by the Houston Astros and played 10 seasons in the minor leagues. He appeared in 932 games, batted .271 lifetime, and played on two Tucson (Triple A) championship teams in 1991 and 1993. Massarelli managed for four seasons in the Houston system after retiring and is currently the manager for the Washington Wild Things of the Frontier League where he was named Manager of the Year in 2004. (UAA.)

One of the most successful University of Akron teams ever was the 1996 squad, which finished 37-23 and made the school's first ever NCAA tournament appearance. Brian Petrucci was the team MVP as well as being All-MAC and All-MAC Tournament. Pitcher Dave Yoder was the MAC Tournament MVP. (UAA.)

One of the most recent Zip baseball success stories was that of Youngstown native Mark Malaska. Much like Mike Birkbeck, Malaska was a multiple threat at the University of Akron from 1997 to 2000, excelling both at the mound and at the plate. He was an All-MAC selection as a right fielder and was drafted in the eighth round of the 2000 baseball draft by the Tampa Bay Devil Rays. He made the Devil Ray's major league club in 2003, and the following year he pitched for the Boston Red Sox (where he received a World Series ring as part of the 2004 championship team). During those two years, Malaska put together a record of 3-2 and an ERA of 3.75. After spending the 2005 season with the Pawtucket (Triple A affiliate of the Red Sox), Malaska retired from baseball shortly before the 2006 season. (UAA.)

A unique match up on the 2006 schedule saw National Association of Intercollegiate Athletics school Malone College (located in Canton) versus University of Akron (dark jerseys). Malone's spirit and offensive skills saw them to a 13-12 win in 10 innings at Jackson Field.

Malone's success (seen here against University of Akron at Jackson Field) in 2006 was not just limited to their David over Goliath role in Akron. On May 20, they won the National Christian College Athletic Association national title by beating Spring Arbor University of Spring Arbor, Michigan, 6-0 in the championship game. The 2006 squad finished with a school record overall of 42 wins. Their previous high mark was achieved by the 1993 team that went 36-9-1.

Pat Bangston, a Tallmadge native and graduate of St. Vincent–St. Mary High School, was a right-handed pitcher for Kent State University in the mid-1980s. He holds the Kent State record for career victories (26) and ranks fourth in career strikeouts (212). Bangston made All-MAC honors in three straight years and was elected to first team honors in 1987. After college, Bangston spent five years in the Minnesota Twins organization. Bangston has also been a successful coach, spending 13 years as the pitching coach of Ohio State University's baseball team. With Bangston as pitching coach, the Buckeyes had the lowest ERA in the league five times, while his pitchers received numerous individual awards (10 Pitcher of the Year awards, five elected All-America honors). In 2005, Bangston was hired as head baseball coach of the University of Akron. He was elected to the Kent State University Athletic Hall of Fame in 2004 and the Greater Akron Baseball Hall of Fame in 1991. (KSU.)

Lou Bocci (third row, far left) was a pitcher for Kent State University in the 1950s. During his college career, he set records for strikeouts in a season (75 in 1954), innings pitched in a season (80 in 1954), career strikeouts (216), and career innings pitched (247). Bocci also threw two no-hitters, and allowed only 151 hits during his career. In addition to his individual achievements, Bocci was elected All-MAC second team in 1952, and first team All-MAC in 1953, 1954, and 1956, making him the first player from Kent State to be elected first team All-MAC three times. He was elected to the Kent State University Athletic Hall of Fame in 1982. (KSU.)

Jim Coll played both baseball and football for Kent State University in the late 1940s. As a first baseman, he started every game for three seasons and earned four varsity Ks. His most notable year was in 1949, when he was cocaptain of his team and hit .379. Coll was also an excellent football player, playing left end and earning two varsity Ks. Following graduation, Coll continued playing baseball (for Post 1055 and Havre Chevrolet teams) and was a teacher as well as superintendent for Ravenna schools. He was elected to the Kent State University Athletic Hall of Fame in 1995. (KSU.)

Frank Curtiss (left), a native of Ravenna played baseball, football, and basketball at Kent State University from 1925 to 1929. He earned a total of 11 varsity letters (four in baseball, where he was team captain in 1928; four in basketball; and three in football). After graduation, Curtiss spent 40 years at Brush High School as a teacher, coach, and eventually athletic director. He was elected to the Kent State University Athletic Hall of Fame in 1980. (KSU.)

Marty Kane was a left-handed pitcher for Kent State University in the late 1950s. In his junior year (1959), Kane led the MAC in ERA and strikeouts and was selected to the All-America MAC first team. In his senior year, Kane was team captain and was once again selected to the All-America MAC first team and led the MAC in strikeouts. In his four years, Kane had 200 strikeouts, averaging more than one strikeout per inning. Following graduation, he played for Boston Red Sox minor league teams such as Olean, New York; Waterloo, Iowa; and Winston-Salem, North Carolina. After retiring from baseball, Kane embarked on a long and storied educational and coaching career. He first started as an assistant baseball coach and English teacher at Parma High School in the early 1960s. This was followed by a 27-year absence from coaching in order to focus solely as a school administrator, holding such jobs as assistant principal at Normandy High School, and principal at Rocky River High School and Kent Roosevelt High School. In 1991, Kane returned to coaching when he accepted the position of head baseball coach at Normandy High School. While coaching, Kane also worked as the director of the Educational Administration program at Ursuline College. He retired from coaching in 2003, but remains at Ursuline College. Kane was elected to the Kent State University Athletic Hall of Fame in 1997. (KSU.)

Gene "Stick" Michael was born in Kent on June 2, 1928. He attended Kent State University, where he lettered in both basketball (1958) and baseball (1958). Although he was given the opportunity to play for the New York Knicks after graduating from Kent State, Michael opted to play baseball instead. He signed with the Pittsburgh Pirates in 1959, making it to the major leagues with the team in 1966. The following year, Michael was traded to the Los Angeles Dodgers for Maury Wills. From 1968 to 1974, Michael played for the New York Yankees, before retiring as a Detroit Tiger after the 1975 season. Primarily a shortstop, Michael earned his nickname due to his skinny frame (6 feet 2 inches, 183 pounds). He also has the distinction of pulling off the "hidden ball" trick five times during his career. (KSU.)

After his playing days ended in 1975, Gene Michael managed the New York Yankees from 1981 to 1982, followed by the Chicago Cubs from 1986 to 1987. In 1990, Michael became general manager of the New York Yankees, where he gained a reputation as a nurturer of talent as opposed to trading young players for proven veterans. This philosophy can be seen with his draft picks, which include such superstars as Bernie Williams, Derek Jeter, Andy Pettitte, and Jorge Posada. In 1996, Michael left his general manager position in order to become vice-president of major league scouting for the Yankees. Six years later, Michael was promoted to vice president and senior advisor of the club. He was elected to the Summit County Sports Hall of Fame in 1980, followed by the Portage County Hall of Fame in 1987. Michael was also inducted into the Kent State University Hall of Fame in 1985. (KSU.)

Thurman Munson was born in Akron and was not only one of the best catchers of his day but arguably one of the best catchers in baseball history. He attended Canton Lehman High School prior to attending Kent State University. While at Kent, Munson was named an All-American catcher in 1968. He then went on to spend the rest of his career with the New York Yankees. His first major league game came in August 1969, when the Yankees were in a transition period that led to the resurrection of another Yankee dynasty of which Munson played an integral part. In 1970, Munson was named American League Rookie of the Year. In 1976 he became the MVP and in his career won three Gold Gloves. Although he spent most of his career playing catcher, he did play a few games as designated hitter, outfielder, first baseman, and one game at third. Thurman was named the first Yankee captain since hall of famer Lou Gehrig. During Munson's 11 years with the Yankees, he was chosen to play in seven all-star games. (KSU.)

Sporting the number 15 on his Yankee pinstripes, along with his leadership abilities, sideburns, and mustache, Thurman Munson was a throwback player who helped the Yankees achieve three American League Championships and three World Series appearances (1976–1978). After losing the World Series in 1976 to the Reds, the Yankees defeated the Dodgers the next two years. Thurman played for owner George Steinbrenner and manager Billy Martin. Some of the cast of characters with whom Munson played included Chris Chambliss, Willie Randolph, Bucky Dent, Graig Nettles, Reggie Jackson, Mickey Rivers, Ron Guidry, Don Gullett, Catfish Hunter, Sparky Lyle, Goose Gossage, Bobby Murcer, and Lou Pinella, just to name a few. Munson's number 15 was retired by the Yankees. His number is one of 15 numbers that have been retired and he is one of 16 Yankee players to receive this honor. Bill Dickey and Yogi Berra each had the number 8 retired. In 1979, Munson's life and career sadly came to a tragic end when he was flying a Cessna jet that crashed at the Akron-Canton Airport. The entire Yankee team came to pay their respects to the captain of the Yankees. The team left his locker empty as a sign of respect. This great catcher is a likely future hall of famer. (KSU.)

Munson made many exciting plays on both offense and defense with the New York Yankees before his untimely death in 1979. In the above photograph, Yankee owner George Steinbrenner and club president Gabe Paul cheer Munson after his game-winning run in a 1977 game. The bottom photograph shows Munson's defensive skills as he fields a ball from Chris Chambliss, forcing out John Ellis. (CSU.)

Matt Resick was the coach of the Kent State baseball team from 1949 to 1961. During that time, the team compiled a 132-100-1 record, with 10 winning seasons (out of 13). Furthermore, 10 of his players went on to play major league baseball, including Gene Michael and Rich Rollins. While serving as the baseball coach, Resick was also a professor and associate dean in Kent's school of health, physical education and recreation (from 1948 to 1975). He has received several honors for his lifetime work, including the Alumni Achievement Award as well as the Outstanding Health and Physical Education Alumni Award, both from Ashland College in 1971 and 1978, respectively. Resick was also inducted into Kent State University Athletic Hall of Fame in 1998. (KSU.)

Rich Rollins played second base for Kent State University in the late 1950s. A graduate of Parma High School, Rollins has the second-best batting average in school history (.389, second to Thurman Munson's .390). He was elected All-MAC second baseman three times (1958–1960), as well as being a three-year letterman. Rollins was signed as an amateur free agent in 1960 by the Washington Senators, which promptly moved to Minnesota and was renamed the Twins. He became the starting third baseman for the Twins in 1962 and was elected American League Rookie of the Year with a batting average of .298, 16 home runs, and 96 RBIs. Rollins played for the Twins for eight years and helped them reach the 1965 World Series against the Los Angeles Dodgers. He spent the last two years of his career playing for the Seattle Pilots (1969), Milwaukee Brewers (1970), and Cleveland Indians (1970). In his 10-year career, Rollins had a career batting average of .269 and hit 77 home runs. He was elected to the Kent State University Athletic Hall of Fame in 1979 and the Greater Akron Baseball Hall of Fame in 2001. (KSU.)

Steve Stone was born on April 8, 1951 in Euclid and attended Brush High School (in Lyndhurst). A right-handed pitcher, Stone attended Kent State University and played two years with the baseball team along with future baseball-great Thurman Munson. He posted a 6-5 win-loss record and a 2.63 ERA in his 18 games with the team, and he was elected first-team All-MAC in 1968. In 1969, Stone was drafted in the fourth round by the San Francisco Giants, and made his major league debut a mere two years later. After two years with the Giants, where he posted an ERA of 4.15 and 2.98 respectively, Stone was traded to the Chicago White Sox, who then traded him a year later to the rival Chicago Cubs. Three years later, Stone rejoined the White Sox for another two years. (KSU.)

TAD

Stone's best years were with the Baltimore Orioles, which he joined in 1979 as a free agent. With the Orioles, Stone won the Cy Young Award in 1980 with a 25-7 record and ERA of 3.23. Unfortunately the next year Stone suffered from tendonitis in his pitching arm, forcing him to spend time on the disabled list and to ultimately retire at the end of the year. Since his retirement, Stone spent 20 years (1983–2000, and 2003–2004) as a color commentator for WGN Chicago, television home of the Chicago Cubs. He was known during his tenure as being outspoken and for having the ability to predict the action before it happened. After leaving WGN at the end of the 2004 season, Stone was hired in 2005 by WSCR Chicago radio to host a weekly talk show as well as by ESPN as a baseball analyst. Stone is a member of both the Kent State University Athletic Hall of Fame (class of 2003) and a 2004 inductee into the International Jewish Sports Hall of Fame, where he ranks third in career wins (107) and strikeouts (1,065). (KSU.)

Alexander Whyte (below, far left in white shirt in team photograph) was the first baseball and basketball coach at Kent State University in the second decade of the 20th century. As a basketball coach, he had a .714 winning percentage from 1913 to 1915. While coaching, Whyte was also a school custodian and helped form the first fraternity on campus (Kappa Mu Kappa, now known as Delta Upsilon). He was elected to the Kent State University Athletic Hall of Fame in 1979. (KSU.)

The Kent State Flashes play home games at Schoonover Stadium. The stadium was named after Harold (class of 1949) and June Schoonover of Akron. Both have been supporters of Kent State for more than 50 years. More than half ($1.53 million) of the $3 million price tag was donated by the Schoonover family, the largest single donation ever to the athletic department. The ceremonial groundbreaking took place on November 25, 2003, with the actual construction beginning in the spring of 2004. The stadium opened in 2005 with 1,148 seats and FieldTurf playing surface. Other features of the stadium include a public plaza; a display area for historical memorabilia; new bull pens, dugouts, and scoreboard, an underground drainage and sprinkler system; and new field lighting and public address system.

The 2006 Kent State University squad went 38-19 and won the MAC regular season title. The team featured four players who were picked in the major league draft in June. Here the University of Akron and Kent State University teams wait through a rain delay. By the third inning, the 9-4 lead the Zips had built was washed away.

4

The Many Faces of Baseball

There are many different faces of baseball. It is not enough to call baseball America's pastime. Fans, owners, players, and businesses all get in on the act. Baseball is all around, even during the off season. It is never more evident than right here in the Akron-Canton area. There is seemingly an endless array of topics from which to choose in an effort to demonstrate the area's involvement. From the days of the industrial leagues, to the interest in dormant stadiums, to collectables, to winning trophies, baseball has entered into the vernacular, clothing, and blood of the area. It is a way of life that is passed down from one generation to another. There are very few sports that fans are willing to listen and thus paint a vivid picture in their mind, without actually seeing it, other than baseball. A season of 162 games catches the imagination enough where one is glued to every game and then talks about it every day. *Akron-Canton Baseball Heritage* gives a unique opportunity to take a glimpse beyond the major league level of the game, with a more intuitive feel for other aspects that envelop the people of this region. There are many ways to be a part of this game besides playing at the big-league level. Baseball, and how it touches lives, brings a smile to young people, the elderly, and all people in between. Not only will this chapter further inspire the love of the game, but hopefully it will get the reader to watch a vintage baseball game at least once. It will bring pleasure with reading about the local history of the game and ballparks in the area as well as increasing the desire to visit them. The captions regarding other ways to participate in the game through umpiring, playing softball, or collecting memorabilia, the authors hope will continue to feed the fervor that already exists. Anyone who had the opportunity to make a great catch, throw a strikeout, or hit a home run knows that special feeling, which is an euphoric rush of invincibility that fills the spirit in a way that words fail to accurately describe.

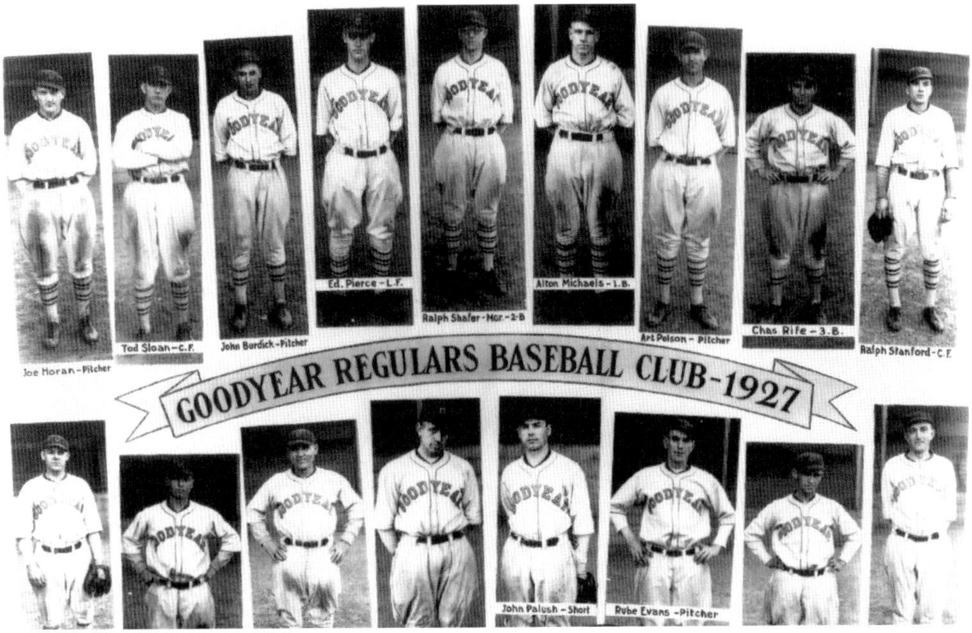

When one thinks of a company team playing ball nowadays, they are liable to think of a loosely organized softball team. Seventy years ago it meant something quite different. Goodyear, Firestone, and a number of other local companies fielded baseball teams that were good enough to play major league exhibition games and hold their own. Shown here is the 1927 Goodyear team, which posted a 19-17-1 record. (UAA.)

Also like professional ballplayers, the Goodyear teams posed for individual pictures as well. This batting stance and swing are of a unique era in baseball. Notice the bat sitting on the batter's shoulder prior to swinging. This was a requirement in the 1800s. This type of stance was more modern and eventually led to the swing that is used today. Shown here is the leading hitter in 1931, right fielder Charley Rife. (UAA.)

On September 12 and 13, 1931, the Goodyear Regulars (above) played the Clearwater Cotton Mill No. 1 of Cedartown, Georgia (below), for the All-Goodyear baseball championship at Seiberling Field. Goodyear won both games, by a score of 5-4 in the first game (helped by a three hit game by Charley Rife) and 6-2 in the second game. (UAA.)

Shown here is the 1932 Goodyear team with manager Smiley Weltow (second row, left). As the picture shows, the city was growing up with baseball and industry. It was a perfect match. Even though they may be smiling for this picture, it was all business on the field. (UAA.)

Goodyear Regulars, 1931 Industrial Champions

PLAY AT HOME EVERY SUNDAY

Goodyear—	1	2	3	4	5	6	7	8	9	R	H	E
Rife, rf												
Porosky, cf												
Pierce, 1b												
Rush, 3b												
Tankersley, 2b												
Nizder, ss												
Clifford, lf												
Case, c												
Burdick, p												
Horan, p												
Miller, p												
Stefko												
Thomas												
Totals												

Newcomerstown	1	2	3	4	5	6	7	8	9	R	H	E
Stoker, cf												
Yanai, 2b												
Lyons, rf												
Norman, lf												
Enold, c												
Heister, 1b												
Weidman, 3b												
Loader, ss												
Deeds, p												
Kenney, p												
Moore, p												
Wassem, p												
Totals												

SUNDAY, JUNE 5— McWILLIAMS SURVEYORS (CLEVELAND)
(Squadron Alumni Day)

SUNDAY, JUNE 12—FISHER FOODS (1931 AMATEUR CHAMPIONS OF UNITED STATES)
(Hunting & Fishing Club Day)

SUNDAY, JUNE 19—Goodyear Girls Day. Ladies Free.

THE F. W. ORTH COMPANY

—Service Printing—

WA-5722

Goodyear supplied their teams with official scorecards to keep track of the action. Similar to professional baseball, promotions were also held by the teams in order to attract fans, such as Goodyear Girls Days. (UAA.)

In 1932, Goodyear pitcher Frank Stefko is pictured warming up before a game in the industrial league. Uniforms and gloves have changed quite a bit over time, but the game is still virtually the same. (UAA.)

Goodyear first baseman Ed "Hump" Pierce is seen here in 1932 playing for the industrial leagues that thrived during the 1930s in the Akron area. Although the fields were not always so fancy, the competition was fierce and the talent level was strong. (UAA.)

Glen "Speed" Bosworth became the first player to be recruited to play industrial baseball. He played for such teams as General Tire of the Industrial League as well as the Akron Orphans, which won several championships including the 1945 National Amateur Baseball Federation national championship. At the end of his career he was a major league baseball scout, and entered two halls of fame: the Summit County Hall of Fame in 1957 and the Greater Akron Baseball Hall of Fame in 1984. (HOF.)

Pictured above is the MVP softball trophy for the 1956 Firestone team. The MVP of that game was shortstop/outfielder Thomas George Maroon. Maroon is also in the Golf Hall of Fame for hitting a hole-in-one at Good Park. Winning in this league meant as much to the factory as it did to the players. Bragging rights were very important to all involved. The entire area would check the papers to find out what team won.

Some industrial teams had stadiums built for them and often played in front of sold-out crowds. One such stadium was Firestone Athletic Field, which was dedicated on July 18 and 19, 1925. Over 10,000 fans attended the two-day event that included speeches by Harvey Firestone and Akron mayor D. C. Rybolt. On July 23, Firestone played an exhibition game against the Cincinnati Reds coming up on the short end of the 12-0 final score.

Today Firestone Athletic Field is still very much in use and serves as the home field of the Akron Racers, the 2005 champions of the National Pro Fastpitch League. The site has undergone renovation and is a very pleasant spot to attend a game.

Goodyear's team stadium, named Seiberling Field, cost $60,000 when it was built. The dedication on July 14, 1929 (below), was witnessed by over 8,000 people, the largest crowd to ever see a baseball game in Akron up to that time. Fittingly enough, Goodyear defeated Firestone 7-2 that day. (UAA.)

For those looking for a different style of baseball to watch in northeast Ohio, there are a number of vintage baseball clubs to see. Most teams play by the rules of the game from around 1860—no gloves, a ball caught on one bounce is considered an out, balls are considered fair by where they first hit the ground, as well as several other unique rules. One of the best local vintage baseball teams is the Akron Black Stockings who play their home games on the front lawn at Stan Hywet Hall and Gardens. The club, which was organized in 1995, has also played at a number of interesting away sites, including Cooperstown and New York City.

Besides the players dressing the part (complete with high stockings and bow tie), the umpires also dress for the occasion. Instead of caps and chest protectors, the umpires governed in style, complete with top hat and walking stick. Cursing would cost a man a day's wages (25¢). The umpire made certain to keep the game clean.

Fans also get into the spirit of these games. Rather than sitting in box seats or loges, they bring their own lawn chair and enjoy homemade refreshments (no $4 pop here). In those days, fans would make noise up close and personal. Even today some stadiums and fairs have hundreds of spectators at games.

Instead of million dollar scoreboards equipped with fireworks, the scores at these games are kept simply with a chalkboard by a woman who must certainly know the ins and outs of baseball. A player rings a bell at the scorer's table to count the run.

Shown here are two of the most potent forces in the Black Stockings lineup: father and son combination of Steve and Rich Paschen. This is truly a game that all generations can enjoy. Whether playing or watching vintage baseball, it brings a smile to the faces of all involved.

The Greater Akron Baseball Hall of Fame was the brainchild of Rudy Piekarski, who played baseball at St. Mary Grade and High School and at the University of Akron. He also managed several Double A ball teams, and ultimately served as commissioner of the Greater Akron Double A baseball league from 1981 to 1992. His idea was to honor players, coaches, managers, umpires, and sponsors who had extraordinary careers in either A, Double A, or the old industrial leagues of Akron. Named the Greater Akron Class A-AA Baseball League Hall of Fame, the organization inducted its first eight members on May 8, 1982, at Anthe's Restaurant on West Market Street in downtown Akron. Two years later, the trustee members voted to change the name to Greater Akron Baseball Hall of Fame in order to honor all of baseball in Akron, regardless of level. (HOF.)

In 1996, the Greater Akron Baseball Hall of Fame was awarded a room at Canal Park (home of the Akron Aeros Double A baseball team). Sharing its space with the Radio-Television Broadcasters Hall of Fame since 2003, memorabilia from both organizations is on display for fans during Aeros games from 90 minutes before the start until the end of the first inning. A minimum of eight individuals are elected each year to the hall of fame, with 60 percent of the votes cast needed for selection. Those who are elected are honored at the annual awards banquet held in the fall. The hall of fame has over 300 inductees and is a must-see for anyone interested in the history of baseball in the Akron area. (HOF.)

William George Evans, better known as Billy Evans, was an American League umpire from 1906 to 1927 (right in photograph with Roger Peckinpaugh). Although he was born in Chicago in 1884, he moved to Youngstown with his family when his father found work at a Carnegie steel plant. After attending Rayen High School he studied law at Cornell University while he played football and baseball. Evans had many accomplishments throughout his life. One of his claims to fame is that he was the youngest person to ever umpire a major league game. His first game behind the dish came at the age of 22. He was a reporter for the *Youngstown Daily Vindicator.* When an umpire did not show up for a game with Hermitage, Pennsylvania, the Youngstown coach asked him to fill in. Evans was quite talented at umpiring, and at the recommendation of the team and players, American League president Ban Johnson gave him the job. Baseball saw him umpire six different World Series during his career. During one season, he umpired seven doubleheaders in eight days. He also had the pleasure of umpiring a perfect game thrown by Charlie Robertson. (CSU.)

After leaving the ranks of umpiring, Evans went on to become the general manager of the Cleveland Indians from 1927 through 1935 (right in photograph with Ava Bradley). In 1936, he became the farm director of the Boston Red Sox, where he stayed until 1940. In 1941 he found the time to work as the general manager for the Cleveland Rams football team. From 1942 until 1946, Evans served as the president of the Southern Association. His baseball career finished with the Detroit Tigers as the general manager from 1947 through 1951. He was replaced by Charlie Gehringer. Baseball was in Evans's blood. He authored the book, *Umping from the Inside* and entered the National Baseball Hall of Fame in 1973. He was the third umpire ever selected into the hall of fame. Evans was not just a great umpire who wrote a book, but also had a knack to write on a regular basis. He authored many articles and had a column called Billy Evans Says. (CSU.)

Billy Evans was loved for his fairness and integrity (right in photograph with Elmer Layden). He was one of the first umpires to bring diplomacy to the position, but was not afraid to be strong either. He once stood up to the challenge of a fight with Ty Cobb after a game. Cobb was not pleased with a couple of the calls behind home plate. In the early days of baseball, fans and players were very rowdy during games. Sometimes fans would pour onto the field creating mayhem forcing games to be called. Umpiring was not a respected position at the time. Evans was once hospitalized after being struck with a bottle during a game. He was also involved in several controversial calls and rule changes including conferring with the fans for an objective decision and disallowing coaches to help players back to their feet during a play. He worked with many great hall of fame players and had an eye for talent that brought future hall of famers to his teams. One of his first moves was bringing Earl Averill to the Cleveland Indians. He objected to the Red Sox selling Pee Wee Reese to the Brooklyn Dodgers. Evans had a great influence on making baseball what it is today and bringing respect and integrity to the positions of umpire and general manager. (CSU.)

The American Legion Post No. 209 was a strong supporter of youth baseball in the Akron area from the 1940s to the 1960s. From 1948 through 1960, the president of Post No. 209 was Dick Leidig. During his tenure, teams sponsored by Post No. 209 had a combined 346-91 win-loss record, as well as winning state championships in Hot Stove Leagues from 1951 to 1953. Following his term as president, Leidig became the president of the Ohio Hot Stove and Summit Umpires groups, and received numerous awards (including Touchdown Club Achievement Award 1963 and the Summit County Hall of Fame Palich Award in 1999). He was also elected into three halls of fame: Ohio High School Athletic Association (2000), Summit Umpires Hall of Fame (2002), and Greater Akron Baseball Hall of Fame (2003). Post No. 209 itself was inducted into the Greater Akron Baseball Hall of Fame as a sponsor in 1997. (HOF.)

Already a successful businessman as head of the Tramonte Distributing Company in Akron, Jack Tramonte (along with his brother Don), sponsored the Double A Black Label baseball teams of the 1960s. The Labels were one of the strongest baseball teams in that decade, winning eight championships in nine years. Tramonte was also known for his generosity with other Double A teams, supplying them with cash and supplies in order to keep their organizations up and running. Today Tramonte is still involved in the company that he founded and is the sponsor of the Miller Lite Cleveland Classic harness horse race. He was inducted into the Greater Akron Baseball Hall of Fame in 1983. (HOF.)

For awhile, Akron-Canton area fans had to drive to League Park in Cleveland to see a major league game. Cars and superhighways were not commonplace yet. It took awhile to get to the games. A trip to League Park meant dressing up and was treated more like a vacation than a quick trip to a game. League Park was located at the corner of East Sixty-sixth Street and Lexington Avenue. Parts of it still stand there today. It opened May 1, 1891, with wooden seats but shut down for a short time before reopening April 21, 1910, with steel and concrete seats. Initially the park held approximately 9,000 fans. It was later upgraded to hold 21,414 fans. To get to the ball park, most people had to travel on Euclid Avenue, which was a showcase of wealthy people's homes and major shopping sites. The park was in place long before the Indians played ball there. Cy Young (yes the Cy Young) pitched the first game at League Park for the Cleveland Spiders of the National League. Right field had a pre-Green Monster. The wall was 40 feet high and had a 20 foot high screen above it. If the ball came back off of the screen, it was still in play. (CSU.)

The Indians won their first World Series at League Park in 1920 against the Brooklyn Robins (later renamed Dodgers). This photograph shows the celebration after the victory. At that time, the park was called Dunn Field after owner Sunny Jim Dunn. League Park saw the first unassisted triple play in World Series history, which was made by Bill Wambsganss. It also saw the first home run by a pitcher in World Series history, hit by Jim Bagby. One other first for League Park included the first grand slam hit in World Series history, which was hit by Elmer Smith. In 1925, Tris Speaker recorded his 3,000th hit in this ball park. A forerunner of today's all-star game was played here in 1911. In 1929, Babe Ruth hit his 500th home run here. In 1941, Joe DiMaggio set a record by hitting safely in his 56th consecutive game here. League Park was home to the Cleveland Spiders, the Cleveland Naps, and the Cleveland Indians. It was also home to the Cleveland Buckeyes of the Negro American League. (CSU.)

Because of the difficulty of fitting a ballpark between streets, League Park was tilted at a counter-clockwise angle. Only day games were played at the park. Baseball games would be held at Municipal Stadium for night and weekend games for some time. As League Park became older, Cleveland built Cleveland Municipal Stadium in an effort to attract the Olympics in 1932 (seen in this photograph in its inaugural year). Although the Olympics did not come to town, the Indians found the confines of this new state-of-the-art ballpark too large. After a short time at Municipal Stadium, the Indians moved back to League Park. Eventually Bill Veeck brought the team back to Cleveland Municipal Stadium and they stayed there until Jacobs Field opened in 1994. (CSU.)

Thurman Munson Memorial Stadium was opened in Canton in 1989. This ballpark was built in the middle of a neighborhood with one main way in and one main way out. Three teams have called this ballpark their home. The first team making this stadium their home was the Canton-Akron Indians of the Eastern League. They were followed by the Canton Crocodiles and the Canton Coyotes of the Frontier League. The stadium holds a crowd of 5,700 people. This aluminum stadium can be quite loud. It was state of the art for its day as far as minor league stadiums are concerned, and it really packed a crowd. The start of the resurgent minor league phenomena in this area can be attributed to this park. Great players, teams, and fans came to this park on their way to "the show." Many of the Indians players who appeared in World Series games graced this field not even a decade before their names became well-known.

Many Cleveland Indians made rehab pit stops at Thurman Munson ballpark since it was so close to Cleveland. Times sure have changed when one compares the facility the Aeros now have at Canal Park in Akron. The stadium still has much potential, but really needs a little love. It has taken on somewhat of a look of League Park after the Indians left. Left and right fields are 330 feet from the plate. It is 400 feet away to dead center. This stadium brought crowds close enough to the field to hear the players speaking with one another no matter where one sat. It was a true pleasure to see a game here. On occasion games are still held at this park.

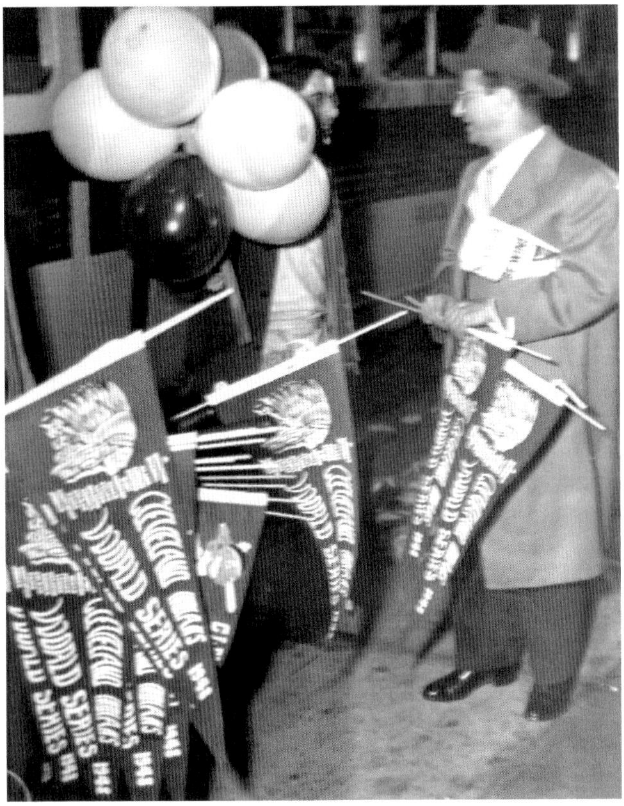

As if baseball games were not entertaining enough, side shows and events fill local parks all across the country in an effort to keep fans entertained between innings. From the big leagues to the local parks, fans cheer on mascots, dance teams, musical chairs, spinning on bats, and hot dog races to occupy their time. In Akron, it is not uncommon to see the batboys dance in the seventh inning or to see children and adults waiving a pennant. Bobblehead stands are as busy as the food lines. (CSU.)

Caution, bleachers may be hot! No this is not a McDonald's coffee warning, it is a known fact around town and at many minor league ballparks across the country. Both Canal Park and Thurman Munson stadium have metal bleachers. On a hot day, wearing shorts can be painful. The fans do not seem to mind at this Aeros game. A regular following meets out there each game hoping to catch a home run off of a player who is hot.

The old adage, "It takes a village to raise a baby" is just as true about baseball as it is about a baby. Minor league owners search the entire country to find fanatics who will support their team. The Akron-Canton area fans have been chosen to support the Aeros, the Captains, the Scrappers, and the Indians. The fan base is very large and quite involved from volunteers who work the games to season ticket holders who support their players no matter what.

Sun.	Mon.	Tues.	Wed.	Thurs.	Fri.	Sat.
	1	2	3	4	5	6
7	8	9	10 AL.-COL. 7:05 PM	11 AL.-COL. 7:05 PM	12 N. BRI. 7:05 PM	13 N. BRI. 1:35 PM
14 N. BRI. 1:35 PM	15	16 LON. 7:05 PM	17 LON. 7:05 PM	18 LON. 7:05 PM	19 WIL. 7:05 PM	20 TV WIL. 7:10 PM
21 WIL. 1:35 PM	22	23 READ. 7:05 PM	24 READ. 7:05 PM	25	26 READ. 7:05 PM	27 READ. 7:05 PM
28 READ. 1:35 PM	29 HARRIS. 7:05 PM	30 HARRIS. 7:05 PM	**APRIL**			

Sun.	Mon.	Tues.	Wed.	Thurs.	Fri.	Sat.
MAY			1 HARRIS. 7:05 PM	2 HAGER. 7:05 PM	3 HAGER. 7:05 PM	4 HAGER. 7:05 PM
5 HAGER. 1:35 PM	6 HARRIS. 7:05 PM	7 HARRIS. 7:05 PM	8 HARRIS. 7:05 PM	9 HAGER. 7:05 PM	10 TV HAGER. 7:10 PM	11 HAGER. 7:05 PM
12 HAGER. 1:35 PM	13	14 AL.-COL. 7:05 PM	15 AL.-COL. 7:05 PM	16 AL.-COL. 7:05 PM	17 N. BRI. 7:05 PM	18 N. BRI. 7:05 PM
19 N. BRI. 1:35 PM	20 WIL. 7:05 PM	21 WIL. 7:05 PM	22 WIL. 7:05 PM	23	24 LON. 7:05 PM	25 LON. 7:05 PM
26 LON. 1:35 PM	27	28 AL.-COL. 7:05 PM	29 TV AL.-COL. 7:10 PM	30 AL.-COL. 7:05 PM	31 N. BRI. 7:05 PM	

All home games played at Thurman Munson Memorial Stadium (Exit 103 off Interstate 77).
Eastern League rules do not permit food or beverage to be brought into stadium.

☐ **HOME** ☐ AWAY **TV Games on WOAC 67**

Sun.	Mon.	Tues.	Wed.	Thurs.	Fri.	Sat.
JUNE						1 N. BRI. 7:05 PM
2 TV N. BRI. 1:40 PM	3 N. BRI. 7:05 PM	4 LON. 7:05 PM	5 LON. 7:05 PM	6 LON. 7:05 PM	7 WIL. 7:05 PM	8 WIL. 7:05 PM
9 WIL. 1:35 PM	10 READ. 7:05 PM	11 READ. 7:05 PM	12 TV READ. 7:10 PM	13 READ. 7:05 PM	14 HARRIS. 7:05 PM	15 HARRIS. 7:05 PM
16 HARRIS. 1:35 PM	17 READ. 7:05 PM	18 READ. 7:05 PM	19 READ. 7:05 PM	20 READ. 7:05 PM	21 HAGER. 7:05 PM	22 HAGER. 7:05 PM
23 HAGER. 1:35 PM	24 TV HARRIS. 7:10 PM	25 HARRIS. 7:05 PM	26 HARRIS. 7:05 PM	27 HAGER. 7:05 PM	28 HAGER. 7:05 PM	29 TV HAGER. 7:10 PM

Sun.	Mon.	Tues.	Wed.	Thurs.	Fri.	Sat.
June 30 HAGER. 1:35 PM	1 AL.-COL. 7:05 PM	2 (2) AL.-COL. 6:05 PM	3 AL.-COL. 7:05 PM	4 N. BRI. 7:05 PM.	5 N. BRI. 7:05 PM.	6 N. BRI. 7:05 PM
7 N. BRI. 1:35 PM	8 N. BRI. 7:05 PM	9	10	11 WIL. 7:05 PM	12 WIL. 7:05 PM	13 WIL. 7:05 PM
14 WIL. 1:35 PM	15 LON. 7:05 PM	16 TV LON. 7:10 PM	17 LON. 7:05 PM	18 TV AL.-COL. 7:05 PM	19 AL.-COL. 7:10 PM	20 (2) AL.-COL. 6:05 PM
21 AL.-COL. 1:35 PM	22 N. BRI. 7:05 PM	23 N. BRI. 7:05 PM	24 N. BRI. 7:05 PM	25 LON. 7:05 PM	26 LON. 7:05 PM	27 LON. 7:05 PM
28 LON. 1:35 PM	29 TV WIL. 7:10 PM	30 (2) WIL. 6:05 PM	31 WIL. 7:05 PM	**JULY**		

Sun.	Mon.	Tues.	Wed.	Thurs.	Fri.	Sat.
AUGUST				1 READ. 7:05 PM	2 READ. 7:05 PM	3 TV READ. 7:10 PM
4 READ. 1:35 PM	5 HARRIS. 7:05 PM	6 HARRIS. 7:05 PM	7 HARRIS. 7:05 PM	8 HARRIS. 7:05 PM	9 READ. 7:05 PM	10 READ. 7:05 PM
11 READ. 1:35 PM	12 HAGER. 7:05 PM	13 HAGER. 7:05 PM	14 HAGER. 7:05 PM	15 TV HARRIS. 7:10 PM	16 HARRIS. 7:05 PM	17 HARRIS. 7:05 PM
18 HARRIS. 1:35 PM	19 HAGER. 7:05 PM	20 HAGER. 7:05 PM	21 AL.-COL. 7:05 PM	22 AL.-COL. 7:05 PM	23 AL.-COL. 7:05 PM	24 N. BRI. 7:05 PM
25 N. BRI. 7:05 PM	26	27 WIL. 7:05 PM	28 WIL. 7:05 PM	29 WIL. 7:05 PM	30 LON. 7:05 PM	31 LON. 7:05 PM

Sun.	Mon.	Tues.	Wed.	Thurs.	Fri.	Sat.
1 LON. 1:35 PM	2 LON. 1:35 PM	**SEPT. Eastern League Playoffs**				

For information call (216) 456-5100

Eastern League Teams

ALBANY-COLONIE YANKEES	CANTON-AKRON INDIANS
HAGERSTOWN SUNS	HARRISBURG SENATORS
LONDON TIGERS	NEW BRITAIN RED SOX
READING PHILLIES	WILLIAMSPORT BILLS

Ticket Prices: $5.00/reserved,
$4.00/general admission,
$2.00/children (14 & under) &
senior citizens, Golden Buckeye card honored

The Eastern League teams that came through Canton were loaded with up and coming major-league talent. Area fans are always wondering what phenom they will be watching next. They all wish to find the next great player and tell anyone who will listen, "I saw him play when." This schedule shows the 1991 season at Thurman Munson stadium for the Double A Indians. WOAC 67 used to be the television home of the team. Even special events nights gave away decent gifts one would not expect to see at a minor-league game in those days.

Fans want to have a piece of the game. Part of doing that is collecting memorabilia from local fan favorites such as Hal Naragon, Joe Charboneau, Mike Hargrove, Herb Score, and many others. Naragon was no slouch, but Charboneau (1980), Hargrove (1974), and Score (1950) were all American League Rookie of the Year winners. Autographed baseball and baseball card shows fill the local malls during the off-season in the area. The fever of collecting pieces of the game is loved at every age level.

The Greater Akron Baseball Hall of Fame not only displays photographs and descriptions of players, umpires, and other baseball personnel, but also houses memorabilia dating back to the industrial leagues. Players wore their baseball affiliation with pride on their jackets and shirts. Shown here are a patch and jacket from championship Akron teams in 1957 and 1952, respectively. (HOF.)

Local high schools have storied baseball programs through the years. The uniforms may change, but the passion these youngsters possess stays the same as the talent improves. Shown here are uniforms from two of Akron's more successful high school baseball programs: Copley High School and Barberton High School. Copley High School is the home of former professional baseball player Jeff Tabaka, and Hal Naragon attended Barberton High School. (HOF.)

George Ellis was an umpire in the Double A Akron leagues for 11 years, where he gained a reputation as being one of the best umpires in the area. Ellis also umpired college baseball games in the MAC and Big Ten Conferences as well. Once his umpiring skills became well known, Ellis was offered umpiring jobs in basketball and football, which eventually led him to the National Football League. Unfortunately Ellis's career was cut short by cancer, and he passed away in 1974 at the age of 54. Ellis was inducted into the Summit County Hall of Fame in 1978 and the Greater Akron Baseball Hall of Fame in 1996. (HOF.)

Originally from West Virginia, Hulbert Hickman started playing baseball in Akron for the North Akron Merchants and Cuyahoga Falls Majestics. He soon joined the mighty Killian Celtics in 1934 as their second baseman. With the Celtics, Hickman gained the reputation as a strong singles hitter who could always be counted on in the clutch. In fact, for all the years that founder Frank Killian fielded a team, Hickman was their only second baseman. He helped the Celtics win the Northern Ohio and Akron-Barberton League Championships and led the team to strong performances in the National Amateur Baseball Federation tournaments. Hickman was inducted into the Greater Akron Baseball Hall of Fame in 1986. (HOF.)

John Hoover started his baseball career playing outfield at Copley High School, where he was elected all-state in 1966. He played baseball for the University of Akron from 1969 to 1970, leading the team in home runs and RBIs during those years and earning team MVP honors in 1969. After college, Hoover played 19 years for Double A Akron baseball teams such as Airmatic Valve, Black Labels, Red Pepper, Forest City, and Crocker Restaurant. During his impressive career, Hoover lead the Double A league twice in home runs, four times in RBIs, and won one batting title. He also was elected to play in 15 all-star games. Once his playing career was over, Hoover began umpiring baseball games in the Akron area. Hoover was inducted into the Greater Akron Baseball Hall of Fame in 1992. (HOF.)

Don Miller began playing baseball at South High School, where he earned three varsity letters as the starting second baseman. Miller attended the University of Akron, but a year later he enlisted in the Army Air Corps. He continued playing baseball in the Army Air Corps while training as a bombardier at Sioux Falls, South Carolina. After his army service, Miller reenrolled at the University of Akron and then signed with the New Castle Chiefs (a Cleveland Indians affiliate in the Penn State League). However, Miller soon went back to Akron to enroll in law school and play Double A baseball for the Hoe Winkler's Civitan Club, Souvenir Beers, Norka Plating, and Ravenna Chevrolet. In his nine-year Double A career, Miller was a two-time all-star and a member of five championship teams. Miller was inducted into the Greater Akron Baseball Hall of Fame in 1997. (HOF.)

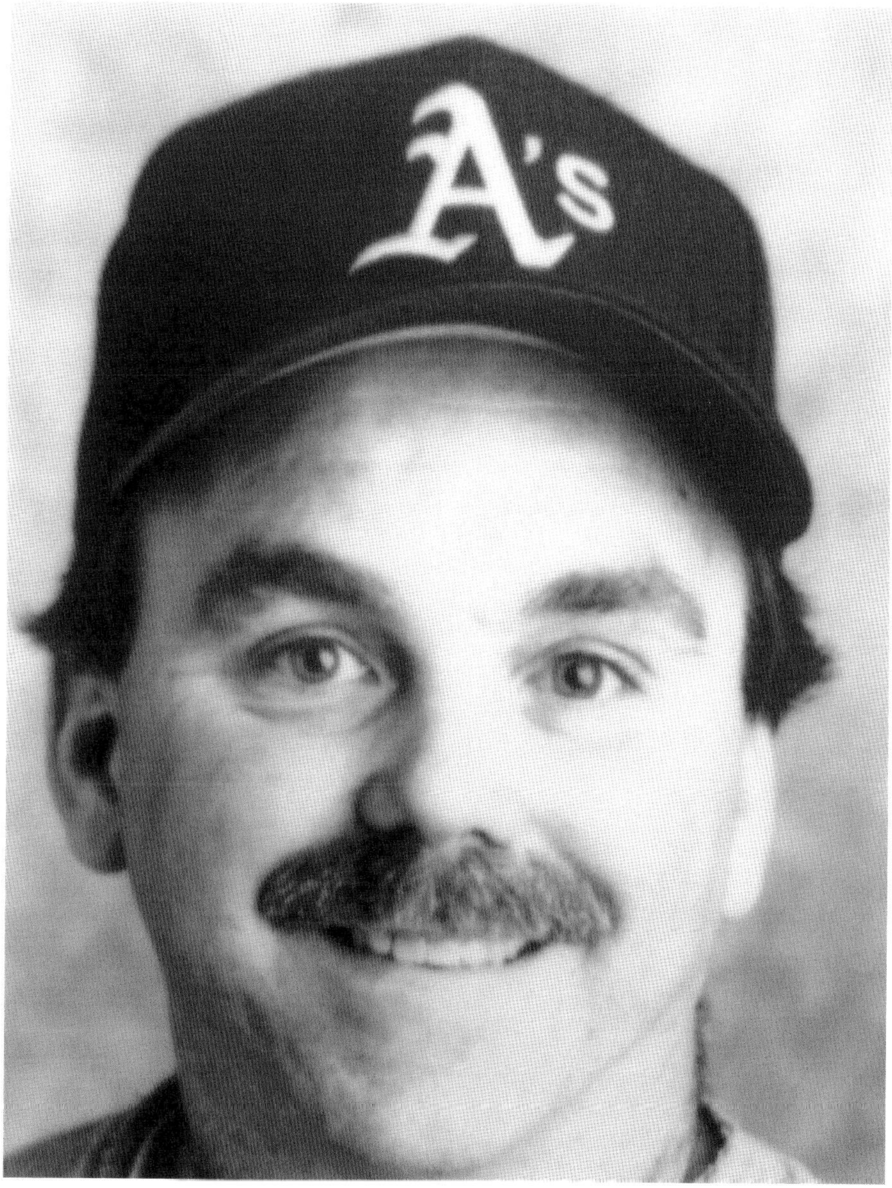

Joe Nauer started pitching as a youth in the South Akron Little League before attending Kenmore High School. While at Kennmore, he helped the baseball team win the 1978 city championship and was elected twice to the all-city team. After high school, Nauer attended Wooster College, where he helped the baseball team win two Ohio Conference titles and was elected to the all-conference team. Upon graduation, Nauer played 15 years in Double A Akron baseball league for the Crocker Restaurant baseball team (winning three titles in five years), the Field Falcons (winning two championships in 1984 and 1985), and the final eight years with the C&P Sales Company. While with C&P, Nauer won four league titles (1986, 1991–1993). He also was elected to eight all-star teams and in 1985, won the Frank Garcia award for outstanding league play. Nauer was inducted into the Greater Akron Baseball Hall of Fame in 1997. (HOF.)

Jack Nicholas (not to be mistaken for the famous professional golfer) played Little League baseball with the Killian Celtics B team and the North High Teens (1939–1940) as well as high school baseball at North High (1941–1942). After graduating from the University of Akron in 1948, Nicholas played Double A baseball in Akron with such teams as the Civitan Club (1945–1948, never missing a game), Norka Plating (1949–1950), Souvenir Beer (1950), Krumroy Markets (1951–1952), and the Red 1 Golf (1953). Overall, Nicholas had a career batting average of .324 and averaged 20 stolen bases per year. Following his playing career, Nicholas turned his attention to coaching. He started out as the assistant basketball coach at North High from 1948 to 1949 and then coached West High from 1951 to 1954. Nicholas then became head baseball coach of West High from 1951 to 1954. From 1954 to 1964, Nicholas headed the Firestone Park Lucky Baseball League for 6- to 10-year-old boys. Later in his career, Nicholas became superintendent of Coventry schools and Revere schools, implementing a strong baseball presence in their athletic programs. Nicholas was inducted into the Greater Akron Baseball Hall of Fame in 1993. (HOF.)

Born in Cleveland, Ohio, Rick Rembielak played Little League ball at Morgana Park along with other Little League teams. He attended Central Catholic High School in Cleveland, where he was awarded all-conference honors in three out of the four years he played baseball. After high school, Rembielak attended Miami (Ohio) University and played shortstop for their baseball team from 1979 to 1981. During his time with the team, Rembielak helped lead the team to an MAC title in 1979 and an appearance in the conference playoffs in 1981. Rembielak was drafted in the 13th round by the Baltimore Orioles in 1981. While never making it to the major leagues, Rembielak spent nearly seven years with the minor league affiliates of the Baltimore Orioles, Chicago Cubs, and Milwaukee Brewers. In 1988, Rembielak left his playing career behind him and became the assistant baseball coach at Kent State University. He became the head baseball coach at Kent State University in 1994, where he compiled a win-loss record of 373-251 from 1994 to 2005; was named MAC Coach of the Year in 1996, 2000, and 2003; and won four MAC regular season championships and three MAC tournament titles. Rembielak left Kent State University in 2004 as the winningest coach at Kent State in any sport. Rembielak was inducted into the Greater Akron Baseball Hall of Fame in 1996. (HOF.)